NOAH

His Life and Times

NOAH

His Life and Times

Samuel W Jennings

JOHN RITCHIE
CHRISTIAN PUBLICATIONS

John Ritchie Ltd.
40 Beansburn, Kilmarnock, Scotland

ISBN 0 946351 44 9

Copyright © 1994 John Ritchie Ltd
40 Beansburn, Kilmarnock, Scotland

All rights reserved. No part of this publication may be reproduced in any form or by any means without prior permission of the copyright owner.

Cover picture Mount Ararat, Turkey
Picture courtesy of the Turkish Tourist Office, London

Typeset by EM-DEE Productions, Glasgow
Printed by Bell & Bain Ltd., Glasgow

Contents

	Page
Introduction	1

Chapter
1. The Structure of Genesis 7
2. Noah in Genesis 17
3. Noah in the Prophets 24
4. Noah in Matthew's Gospel 33
5. Noah in the Gospel of Luke 38
6. Noah in Hebrews 11 48
7. The Seven Points of Noah's Faith 52
8. References to Noah in 1 Peter 60
9. The Flood in 2 Peter 67
10. Spiritual Truth in Noah 75
11. Baptism in 1 Peter 3 84
12. The Evil People of Genesis 4 89
13. The Spiritual Man of Genesis 5 98
14. The Corrupt Generation of Genesis 6 106
15. The Sons of God 111
16. The Evil Generation of Genesis 6-8 119
17. A Passage in Job 126
18. Noah the Man 130
19. The Godly Man 139
20. The Two Natures 149
21. The Lord Manifested in Genesis 6 155
22. Salvation is of the Lord 162
23. Faithfulness and Food 172
24. The Goodness and Severity of God 177
25. The Faithful Creator in Genesis 8 184
26. The God of all Grace in Genesis 9 192
27. The Everlasting Covenant 199
28. A Dispensational Picture 207

INTRODUCTION

It is customary to present the story of Noah, his ark and the flood, primarily to children. This may be due to the interest which children show in animals. Over the years it has been related to children by both parents and Sunday School teachers. Countless story books have been published depicting Noah as an old man with a long white beard building a "boat" of sorts, which has a house perched on top of it to accommodate the family and many animals peering over the bulwarks.

The tendency to create out of this passage a romantic story for children, means that this part of the Scripture has not been given the place it merits, either in the ministry and reading among the saints, or in private study. Rather it has been consigned to providing amusement for the young until such times as they leave these "childish" things behind them and progress to material considered suitable for the more mature.

This passage of God's word is widely regarded as a mere myth, and is severely criticised by the educated society of our day. The modernist repudiates it, and sincere believers neglect it considering it to be material fit only for children.

NOAH

However, there are four chapters of Genesis devoted to this story. It is therefore equal in length to the epistles to the Colossians and to the Philippians, and indeed to the upper room discourse of our Lord in John chs. 13-16 which is so precious to the Lord's people. In fact one hundred and one verses are devoted to its unfolding— including the last verses of Genesis 5 and all of Genesis chs. 6-9. Such a long and detailed passage, inspired by the Holy Spirit as all Scripture is, cannot be ignored without suffering great loss.

Let us first consider some of the tremendous truths which should fascinate and thrill every child of God, and at the same time make us more sober-minded.

1. In our passage, judgment is passed on all the world. This is the only example from the past of God's righteous judgment upon all mankind.

Judgments have often been made, some of them on a large scale such as God's displeasure upon Israel in the wilderness: in one plague 24000 people perished (Num 25:1-9). Again, in the captivity the whole nation of Israel was judged by the Lord.

Now these judgments were on a national scale, as was the destruction of certain nations that inhabited the land of Canaan, but the Genesis passage records a world- wide catastrophe involving every living creature. "God looked upon the earth, and behold it was corrupt: for all flesh had corrupted his way upon the earth. And God said unto Noah, "The end of all flesh is come before me" (Gen 6:12, 13).

The extent of this judgment is seen in Gen 7:21. "All flesh died that moved upon the earth, both of fowl and of cattle, and of beast, and of every creeping thing that creepeth upon the earth, and every man" . Note the words *all* and *every*. There was no escape except in the

INTRODUCTION

safety of the ark.

Even the salvation by means of the ark is most embracive in its scope. "In the selfsame day entered Noah, and Shem, and Ham, and Japheth, the sons of Noah, and Noah's wife, and the three wives of his sons with him, into the ark: They and every beast after his kind, and every creeping thing that creepeth upon the earth after his kind, and of every fowl after his kind, every bird of every sort. And they went into Noah into the ark, two and two of all flesh, wherein is the breath of life" (Gen 7:13-15).

The apostle Peter found that he could not ignore this world-wide judgment in 2 Peter 3, where he compares the flood event with the judgment by fire that is yet to come upon the earth, drawing parallels between the two.

2. Again, let us note God's favour, and the salvation He offers from that judgment by means of the ark, to which Peter also refers: "eight souls were saved by water". Salvation is seen in the previous chapters of Genesis both in type and experience, but here is a salvation not merely from the jaws of death, but from impending judgment. We must also acknowledge that it is a wondrous display of grace that God should favour man at all.

3. Let us also consider this point: men can shine for God even in the midst of such a corrupt and violent society, and can bring pleasure to the very heart of God. It is possible to shine as a luminary in the midst of a crooked and perverse generation as exhorted in Phil 2:15.

4. Above all else, we can only be amazed at such a display of the faithfulness of God. His covenant is mentioned eight times. This number in Scripture signifies that which is new and eternal, and indeed a reference is made to the "everlasting covenant" (Gen 9:16). Note also the beautiful words "God remembered Noah" (Gen 8:1). Noah and his family are hidden in the ark; the ark is a mere speck upon the mass of waters, yet Noah is seen, known and remembered by God.

5. Another detail worth mentioning is that the flood brought about a dramatic change in God's dealings with man and in man's life upon the earth.

  1. A greater variety of food was provided after the flood and the covenant: God allowed man to eat flesh; until then, man was totally vegetarian.
  2. God promised that the seasons would follow one another without interruption, to the benefit of mankind.
  3. In some measure the curse was lifted from the earth: it was to yield greater increase by cultivation.
  4. To these is added the institution of the death penalty which has been respected by past generations and governments and is now set aside by man to his loss and confusion.

Thus, we are all in some measure affected by the flood and its aftermath.

The history of Noah, the godless times and the resulting flood with all their spiritual implications and import, is authenticated by the references made to it by other Biblical characters, and by the Lord Himself.

  1. "For this is as the waters of Noah unto me: for... I have sworn that the waters of Noah should no more go over the earth" (Isa 54:9).
  2. "Though Noah, Daniel, and Job, were in it, ...they shall but deliver their own souls by their righteousness" (Eze 14:20).
  3. "But as the days of Noah were, so shall also the coming of the Son of man be. For as in the days that were before the flood they were eating and drinking, marrying and giving in marriage, until the day that

INTRODUCTION

Noah entered into the ark, And knew not until the flood came and took them all away" (Matt 24:37-39). A parallel passage may also be found in Luke 17:26-7.

4. "By faith Noah being warned of God of things not seen as yet, moved with fear prepared an ark to the saving of his house: by the which he condemned the world and became heir of the righteousness which is by faith" (Heb 11:7).

5. "The long-suffering of God waited in the days of Noah while the ark was a preparing" (1 Pet 3:20).

"If God...spared not the old world, but saved Noah the eighth person, a preacher of righteousness, bringing in the flood upon the world of the ungodly" (2 Pet 2:5).

"the world that then was being overflowed with water, perished" (2 Pet 3:6).

So we see that two Old Testament prophets, the Lord and two New Testament writers all record that not only did these events take place, but that important lessons can be derived from them by careful study. Let us then turn to the pages of Holy Writ, and reap profit for ourselves from the experience of such a worthy man and his times.

1

THE STRUCTURE OF GENESIS

Genesis has often been called the seed-plot of the Bible, where all the great doctrines in the progressive revelation of Holy Scripture can be seen in germ form. While this is a fact readily acknowledged by all true Bible students, Genesis is primarily a character study.

The book takes in twenty three generations and consequently many names appear, yet all the writing is structured around eight prominent men and their experiences. They are arranged in two groups of four.

Adam, Abel, Enoch, and Noah comprise the first group. Genesis chs. 1-11 span nineteen generations; here we have the story of the nations springing first from Adam, and continuing through to Noah, and life after the flood.

The second group is better known, being of course Abraham, Isaac, Jacob and Joseph. These four generations are covered by God in greater detail than the previous four men and their generations; thirty-nine chapters are devoted to their experiences, that is the whole of chapters 12-50. The chief concern in this section is no longer the nations, but the birth of the nation, Israel. According to God's purpose, this nation would eventually produce the Christ, bringing into existence the Church of God and consequently blessing to both Jew and Gentile.

Some may object that this selection of eight prominent men in Genesis is arbitrary, pointing out that there are hundreds of names and characters in this first book of the Bible. Many of these men are important: Cain, Ishmael,

NOAH

Laban and Esau to name a few. Why single out these eight?

It is evident that the New Testament lays special emphasis on these eight characters. In Heb 11 the worthies of the faith commence with Abel, then proceed to Enoch and Noah, and then to Abraham, Isaac, Jacob and Joseph, omitting all the others found in Genesis. To these we must add Adam, the first man. He does not feature as a man of faith in Heb 11, but he is nonetheless important. Doctrine of a most fundamental nature is drawn from the parallels between Adam and Christ in Rom 5 and 1 Cor 15. The following interesting and important references to these eight men are worthy of consideration.

Adam speaks of headship and the fall. He is a figure of Him that was to come, that is Christ (Rom 5:14).

Abel is described in Heb 11 as a man of faith, the first in whom we see the faith principle in operation, and the first to offer a sacrifice to God. In Heb 12:24 the shedding of his blood by his brother Cain is contrasted with the wilful murder of the Christ by His nation: Abel's blood cried for vengeance, but when God viewed the blood of Christ shed as a sacrifice for sin, it spoke of better things for Israel— grace, peace and salvation.

Enoch is referred to as a man of faith in Heb 11:7 but note that in Jude 14, 15 he was the first preacher in the Bible; he was the first to witness to the Lord's return and the great day of the Lord. Also he was the first man on record to be caught up by God to heaven without dying and the first man in the Bible of whom it is recorded that "he walked with God" (Gen 5:22)

Perhaps Paul had Enoch in mind when writing 1 Thess 4 which begins, "Ye have received of us how ye ought to walk and to please God"; the very words used to describe Enoch in Heb 11:5. In concluding the chapter

THE STRUCTURE OF GENESIS

Paul reveals that we "shall be caught up together to meet the Lord in the air" and that of course is similar to the experience of Enoch.

Noah, as we have already seen and will later discover in greater detail, forms the basis for many important subjects expounded by the New Testament writers.

Abraham, so often mentioned in the New Testament is used by the Holy Spirit in a threefold way.

(a) Dispensationally: the Pharisees said to John the Baptist, "We have Abraham to our father" (Matt 3:9) Being of Abraham, Israel is able to claim the kingdom. Again in Matt 8:11 "Many shall come from the east and west, and shall sit down with Abraham ... in the kingdom of heaven". Note also that the genealogy of the Messiah in chapter one is traced back to Abraham.

(b) Doctrinally: we are justified by faith (Rom chs. 4-5; Gal ch. 3). Zacchaeus was a son of Abraham through the principle of faith. Similarly the Lord described as "a daughter of Abraham" the woman who had been bound by Satan and was loosed (Luke 13:16). We too who believe in Christ are the children of Abraham because of similar faith exercised (Gal 3).

(c) Morally: in John 8:39-40 the Lord refers to the works of Abraham, drawing a contrast between them and the evil thoughts in the hearts of men who opposed Him and sought to kill Him. Again, in v. 56 the Lord says that "Abraham rejoiced to see my day". All these references point to Abraham as an example of moral uprightness. James would agree, making mention of Abraham as the friend of God, and referring to his works (James 2:21-23)

In Galatians we find that the Spirit views Isaac in a twofold way: as a type of Christ, the seed of Abraham, (3:16); and as a type of the believer as born of the Spirit: "Now we brethren, as Isaac was, are the children of

NOAH

promise. But as then he that was born after the flesh (Ishmael), persecuted him that was born after the Spirit (Isaac), even so it is now" (4:28,29).

In Heb 11:20-21 Jacob the pilgrim, as he called himself before Pharaoh, worships leaning upon the top of his staff. Although not mentioned in the other epistles, he is the great example of discipline in the school of God.

Joseph is a wonderful type of Christ, although he is not clearly referred to as such in the New Testament. He too is seen in the hall of fame as a man of faith (Heb 11:22). He is presented as a great believer in resurrection; he did not want to remain buried in Egypt, but gave instruction that his bones were to be buried in the Promised Land, as he wanted to be resurrected from that special place.

So the eight men highlight truths which are precious to the believer as expounded in the New Testament.

In seeking further to prove that the key to the book of Genesis lies in the singling out of these particular eight men to the exclusion of all others, consider the structure of Genesis itself.

The eight histories exhibit what is called inverted parallelism, that is the first and the last have several features in common, similarly the second and the seventh, and so on. Let us consider a few points to illustrate this without going into great detail.

Firstly we have Adam, and Joseph, the first and last men of the eight.

1. One ruled over Eden, the other over Egypt.
2. One was cast out by God, the other had the sad experience of being cast out by his brethren.
3. Both had two sons, and the blessing in each case went to the younger: Abel had preference over Cain; and Ephraim over his brother Manasseh..

THE STRUCTURE OF GENESIS

4. Each had only one wife, and both women are pictures of the church, the bride of Christ.
5. Each had a coat made for him: Adam had a coat of skin made by his Father, God; Joseph had a coat of many colours made for him by his father, Jacob.
6. Death also had a claim upon each in an interesting way. To Adam God said, "For dust thou art, and unto dust shalt thou return" (Gen 3:19). Joseph refers to his bones, not his body (Gen 50:25), and so recognises the dust principle of Genesis ch. 3.
7. But the most striking contrast is to do with the woman, and temptation. Adam was confronted by a woman who tempted him: he succumbed, bringing loss to himself and the world. Joseph was also tempted by a woman standing before him: he fled, thus saving his character, and the testimony of God.

Surely all this is not mere coincidence, but is designed by a careful and all-wise God who displays wisdom in His Word that we might search it out to our profit. The careful reader can no doubt add other contrasts or comparisons.

In the same manner the second and the seventh, Abel and Jacob, can be compared.

1. Abel offered, and Jacob worshipped, leaning on the top of his staff.
2. Abel had a very short life, and Jacob had a very long one. This contrast is seen in two worthies in the New Testament: James was killed in early life by the sword of Herod, his brother John lived to a very ripe old age.
3. Abel was persecuted by his brother Cain, and Jacob feared his brother Esau later in his life.
4. Abel gave gifts to God as recorded in Heb 11:4. Jacob

11

promised gifts to God—a tenth of his goods (Gen 28:22) and ended by giving abundant gifts to Esau!
5. A very conclusive point that draws a parallel between these two is Heb ch. 12 where each one is directly cited as part of a warning passage. "Esau for one morsel of meat sold his birthright" (taken by guile by Jacob) and "he found no place of repentance through he sought it carefully with tears" (Heb 12:16-17). Further down the chapter in v. 24 the blood of Abel is contrasted with the blood of Christ, which "speaketh better things than the blood of Abel".

Thus these two are closely linked by the Spirit of God although they lived centuries apart, and their lives were separated by the flood.

The same pattern comes out in Enoch, the third man, and Isaac who was the fifth. Obvious parallels bring them together.

1. The number seven is associated with both men. Enoch was the seventh generation from Adam (Jude 14) and Isaac was the twenty-first from Adam.
2. In both cases the father was old. Much truth is based upon this fact. Methuselah was the oldest man that ever lived—969 years. He displays the *grace* of God, for his death was God's calendar date for the bringing in of the flood. God takes "no pleasure in the death of the wicked" (Eze 33:11), so Methuselah consequently lived longer than any other man. It perhaps could be said that God was putting off the evil day.

In a greater degree, Abraham, the father of Isaac, manifests the *power* of God, being so old when Isaac was born. Nothing is impossible with God. The message of the angel of the Lord to Sarah was, "Is

THE STRUCTURE OF GENESIS

anything too hard for the Lord?" (Gen 18:14). Later the New Testament declares Isaac "was born after the Spirit" (Gal 4:29).

The great teaching is that to inherit the blessing of heaven a man must be born again, born of the Spirit; natural birth is not enough.

3. Enoch escaped the flood having been raptured, and Isaac escaped the knife of his father, thanks to the ram caught in the thicket. In both cases escape was by reason of God's providing. In fact, the two comings of our Lord Jesus are prefigured in these separate experiences. Isaac and the ram point to His first coming to take the sinner's place on the cross. The rapture of Enoch is a type of the Lord returning to the air, and the catching up of the church to meet Him (1Thess 4:13-18).

Much could be added to this by way of contrast and comparison by the diligent student of Scripture. To some this approach may be uninteresting and unnecessary, seemingly to satisfy the curious mind rather than to feed the soul. However, if one desires to come to an understanding of the Hebrew epistle, it will have to be accepted that contrasting and comparing the old convenant and the new, the priesthood of Aaron and the priesthood of Melchisedec etc. is God's method of presentation in that book.

The same can be said about the four Gospels. The beauty and the great spiritual lessons are seen, not by trying to harmonise the material but rather by contrasting one Gospel with the other. God's word, like all His works, is orderly. One can expect, and look to see, that order emerges in various patterns and structures. Indeed, this is one of the great proofs of inspiration.

The central two men of the eight highlighted in

NOAH

Genesis are Noah, number four, and Abraham number five.

1. A fact not so evident is that both men are tenth generations: Noah being the tenth from Adam, and Abraham being the twentieth. The number ten in the Scriptures speaks of responsibility as in the ten commandments given in Exodus ch. 20. Another occurence is the ten servants of Luke ch. 19. Each is given a pound to trade for his master's use during his absence.

   Truly the responsibility that fell upon the shoulders of both these characters was great. Noah produced an ark. Abraham produced a nation. This is one branch of many in which they bore responsibility, and all by faith (Heb 11:7-19).

2. Again, Noah is the last of the first four representative men before the flood, and Abraham is the first of the last four after the flood; this is most important. The one closes a dispensation, while the other opens a dispensation, that of promise.

3. Again, both were called by God and separated. The first was separated from the old world by water (1 Pet 3:20) while the second was separated from his kindred by the call of God (Gen 12:1-2).

4. It is profitable to observe that the motivating factor in Noah was fear (Heb 11:7), but in the case of Abraham it was the glory of God. "The God of glory appeared unto our father Abraham, when he was in Mesopotamia" was the testimony of Stephen (Acts 7:1-2).

   How true this is of our different experiences in coming to the Living Stone for salvation. In some the motivation has been the fear of the judgment of God, and in others attraction to the grace and glory of God.

THE STRUCTURE OF GENESIS

The Holy Spirit still operates in this way in the gospel today. Either the dread of eternal punishment, or God's love and righteousness move the soul to seek Christ. The fear of sin's consequence, or weariness of sin's practice and power produces a longing for peace and something better until Christ is found.

These two ways can be illustrated in the apostle Paul. As Saul of Tarsus he was attracted to Christ by the glory he saw on the Damascus road. Later he had the joy of seeing the jailor of Philippi saved by fear. Both of them trembled, both were blessed by salvation—the one at midday, the other at midnight.

5. With only these two, of all the characters of Genesis, did God enter into covenant.. Noah's covenant was concerned with the earth and its fruitfulness. Abraham's covenant concerned the land of Canaan, and the possession of it through the promised seed, that is Christ.

It is interesting to observe that a sign of the covenant was given to each. Noah was given the bow in the sky; Abraham was given the circumcision of the body. There is no other such information in the book of Genesis. God is responsible for the first sign, namely the placing of the bow in the sky. Man is responsible for the other—that of the circumcision of the body.

Already God is indicating the basis of His relationship with Israel, that is, obedience to the laws of God. Both of these signs speak of the coming Messiah, the work He would do to redeem man and the manifestation of the character of a faithful Creator.

Nevertheless, both of these men had lapses in their lives. Abraham went down into Egypt; Noah went down into a drunken sleep and brought a curse upon part of his future posterity. (This shall be considered

in greater detail later.)
6. Again, we cannot fail to notice in passing that each had a son, which proved to be a disappointment to him. Noah was disappointed with Ham, while Abraham was disappointed with Ishmael.
7. Note again, as so often in these couplets, that close reference is made to them in the New Testament. First Peter 3 commences: "Sarah obeyed Abraham, calling him lord". This is an example to all godly wives to acknowledge God's appointed headship in the home. The chapter closes with Noah being saved through the waters, an example to all baptized believers to acknowledge Christ as their Lord. "He is gone into heaven, and is on the right hand of God; angels and authorities and powers being made subject unto him" (1 Pet 3:22). He is Lord of all, then how much more is He Lord to the baptized believer?.
8. Another comparison we dare not be miss, is that both of these saints had altars, Abraham had four while Noah had but one. Nevertheless, Noah is the first man in the Bible to build an altar, in this he is original. Noah was the path-finder and Abraham developed what Noah had started. So while one had four altars, and the other had only one, yet that one had the glory of being the first. Perhaps Abel had an altar upon which he offered his sacrifice, but Scripture is silent on this. We must take notice of the silences of Scripture and the law of first mention.

Let us then leave these great men, profitable as they are, and rewarding in study, and let us now consider especially Noah, our subject as he is found in the book of Genesis.

2

NOAH'S PLACE IN GENESIS

Genesis, being a book of beginnings, emphasises genealogies; in fact there are eleven of them. One might refer to them as family trees of a sort. In a beautiful way genealogies are used by the Spirit of God to round off very neatly the record of Noah in the book. One introduces the story of this remarkable man, and another ends the record.

In ch. 5 we read of the genealogy of Adam through Seth; it ends with a reference to the birth of Noah in v. 28, and to his age being 500 years in v. 32. The history closes in 9:29 with his death at the age of 950 years. In ch. 10 a very long genealogy follows, giving the details of his posterity through his three sons. So God encloses the whole story between two genealogies, two mentions of his age, and the record of his birth and his death.

Added to this, a curse begins and ends the history. At his first mention, Lamech said, "This same shall comfort us concerning our work and toil of our hands, because of the ground that the Lord hath cursed"(Gen 5:29). How interesting that the narrative closes with Noah cursing his grandson, Canaan (Gen 9:25).

Alongside this, one will observe that his three sons are mentioned in the commencement (Gen 5:32) and at the close. The last act of Noah before his death was the blessing and cursing of his three sons.

Let us for convenience, put all this in tabular form.

17

NOAH

A. THE BEGINNING OF THE STORY
1. Genealogy of Seth to Noah   Chapter 5
2. Birth of Noah   Chapter 5
3. Some comfort because of curse   Chapter 5
4. Age 500 years   Chapter 5
5. His three sons   Chapter 5

B. THE CLOSE OF THE HISTORY
1. Three sons and their actions   Chapter 9
2. Cursed be Canaan   Chapter 9
3. Age 950 years   Chapter 9
4. Death of Noah   Chapter 9
5. Noah's sons' genealogy   Chapter 10

So all five points in ch. 5 are paralleled in chs. 9,10 and are almost in reverse order. It is therefore plain to see that God is rounding off the story of Noah, setting the narrative between these two sets of parallel thoughts.

The narrative itself circles round three main events.

1. The building of the ark, and the subsequent flood.
2. The building of the altar, and the subsequent covenant.
3. The planting of the vineyard, and the subsequent curse.

This teaches us that actions never terminate in themselves, but have far reaching effects for good or for bad.

1. The ark saved eight people, but the flood destroyed the rest.
2. The altar brought pleasure to God, and also blessing and government to man upon the earth.
3. The vineyard brought present joy in labour, but alas led to drunkenness and disgrace to Noah, blessing to two of his sons, and a curse upon the posterity of the other.

NOAH'S PLACE IN GENESIS

This is a solemn warning to all, and especially to the Christian; everything is so far reaching like a stone cast into a pond, sending ripples to the uttermost banks. The classic case of this principle is Adam "By one man sin entered into the world, and death by sin; and so death passed upon all men for that all have sinned" (Rom 5:12). Truly Rom 14:7 informs us, "For none of us liveth unto himself". The Lord by one act of obedience upon the tree (in contrast with Adam's act concerning another tree) has brought righteousness and blessing to all, who by faith place themselves under His Headship (Rom 5:17-19)

One cannot study the ark and the flood without observing the time notes throughout the story. The periods are marked off by days as follows.

1. "For yet seven days, and I will cause it to rain upon the earth" (Genesis 7:4).
2. "I will cause it to rain upon the earth, forty days and forty nights" (7:4).
3. "And it came to pass after seven days, that the waters of the flood were upon the earth. And the rain was upon the earth forty days and forty nights" (vv. 10,12).
4. "And the waters prevailed upon the earth an hundred and fifty days" (7:24) "After the end of the hundred and fifty day the waters were abated" (8:3).
5. "And it came to pass at the end of forty days that Noah opened the window of the ark which he had made..." (8:6ff).
6. "And he stayed yet other seven days; and again he sent forth the dove out of the ark" (8:10f).
7. "And he stayed yet other seven days; and sent forth the dove; which returned not again to him any more" (8:12).
8. We should also note the time factors that are brought forward in Noah's age. "Noah was six hundred years old when the flood of waters was upon the earth" (7:6). This age is repeated in verse 11. Again, Noah's

19

NOAH

age is referred to in 8:13. "In the sixth hundred and first year...the waters were dried up from off the earth".

From all this we learn that God's times are pre-eminent, in the ark, and the flood.

The altar on the other hand presents God's ways:

1. Noah knew that blood offerings were "normal" with God. This was something that Cain ignored to his cost.
2. He also knew that the offerings had to be clean.
3. He was able to discern what was clean, long before Leviticus 11 was written. He was familiar with God's ways.
4. Again, His ways are unfolded in His communications to Noah issuing from His pleasure in Noah's offering (8:21 9:17).

The vineyard, and the consequent drunkenness was contrary to God's will. Was it God's will that His servant should abuse the produce of the new earth and manifest that fallen nature, bringing a curse upon his grandson? For once, Noah stepped out of God's will. He had neither instruction, as with the ark, nor precedent, as in the offerings. It was something devised in Noah's own heart. This is the seat of the natural man, it cannot please God.

Now all this is quite remarkable, the same ideas permeate the temptations of our blessed Lord in Matthew 4, but in the reverse order.

The first temptation was in the wilderness and concerned the will of God. The Lord had fasted for forty days, and was tempted to command the stones to be made into bread. Of course, our Lord refused because God had given Him no command to do such. So it was an attempt by Satan to turn aside the Son of man from God's will.

The second temptation was that our Lord should act contrary to God's ways. Satan tempted our Lord in the

NOAH'S PLACE IN GENESIS

holy city: standing on the pinnacle of the temple, he said: "Cast thyself down: for it is written he shall give his angels charge concerning thee, and in their hands they shall bear thee up, lest at any time thou dash thy foot against a stone" (Matt 4:6). It is well known that the devil is referring to Ps 91:11-12, but he omitted "in all thy ways". The devil was suggesting a public demonstration of something sensational to affect the crowds that gathered around the temple courts, and to gain support. This would have been easier than the path of suffering, humility, shame, and death, which was God's way.

In the first temptation the circumstances already existed: the Lord was in the wilderness; He was hungry; He had no bread. The second temptation was to manipulate circumstances to His own advantage. This was not God's way. The Lord saw the subtlety of the temptation and replied, "Thou shalt not tempt the Lord thy God" (Matt 4:7).

The third temptation was related to God's time. It was that our Lord should act before the appointed time. Standing on a high mountain, Satan showed the Lord all the kingdoms of this world in a moment of time, saying, "All these things will I give thee". They are the Lord's by right, as is clearly spoken in the prophetic word. "Ask of me, and I shall give thee the heathen for thy inheritance, and the uttermost parts of the earth for thy possession" (Ps 2:8, spoken by God to Christ). The devil said *now*, God said *then*. God's time had not yet come, and the Lord refused.

Eventually all will be His. The reference in Revelation 11:15 says "The kingdoms of this world are become the kingdoms of our Lord, and of his Christ; and he shall reign for ever and ever".

So in the ark, the altar, and the vineyard, are found the three things that test every man. Noah could pass in two, but the Lord gloriously is victor in all three. He was

21

NOAH

the Son of God, but standing upon the earth as the Son of man fulfils all God's will, He fully followed all God's ways, and patiently awaits God's time.

The story of the ark and flood runs from Genesis 6:5 to Genesis 8:22, and again the details are perfectly balanced in inverted parallels. Why does God use this method? Firstly to aid the memory. The Jews memorised the Scriptures extensively upon the command of God. How gracious that the Spirit so inspired the writers to keep to a form and pattern as an aid to the task of committing long passages to memory.

Secondly, to use the centre to highlight some detail, some truth or statement that has no parallel. Now in the case of the record in Genesis 6:5 to 8:22, this parallel structure is definitely placed by the Holy Spirit.

A. The earth is corrupt and violent. God says "I will destroy" (6:5-21)
  B. Noah builds the ark. (6:22)
    C. Come thou and thy house into the ark. (7:1)
      D. Seven days waiting until the flood came. (7:7-10)
        E. Forty days rain upon the earth and the turmoil. (7:10-23)
          F. 150 days that the waters were upon the earth. (7:24)
            G. God remembered Noah. (8:1)
          F. 150 days the waters were abating upon the earth. (8:1-3)
        E. Forty days until the ark rested upon mount Ararat. (8:4-6)
      D. Seven days waiting between sending the dove out on the two occasions. (8:7-12)
    C. God said "Go forth of the ark" (8:16)
  B. Noah builds an altar. (8:20)
A. The Lord said "I will not again curse the ground—Day and night shall not cease". (8:21-22)

Other details fit in just as easily but we do not want the above list to become uncontrollable, or difficult to apprehend. We, must however, add the reference to Noah's age both before and after the given details (7:11 and 8:13)

The centre piece of course is Genesis 8:1, "God remembered Noah". We see God's purpose not only in judgment but also in grace. Noah was very special to the Lord. So every child of God is known and preserved by God in this world of conflict. It is said of the Lord, "Having loved his own which were in the world, he loved them unto the end" (John 13:1).

Indeed the many saints that have already arrived in heaven are not less loved by the Lord, but in a special way He knows and remembers His own in this world, the place of conflict and tribulation. This is a great consolation to every saint that is passing through deep waters of affliction—God remembered Noah.

So in some little way we have sought to discover that what God says in His word is important, but the order in which He says the things is equally important. "God is not the author of confusion, but of peace" (1 Cor 14:40). The exhortation to us is—"rightly dividing the word of truth" (2 Tim 2:15).

3

NOAH AND THE PROPHETS

The histories of many men, some of them the most wonderful of men, appear on the pages of Holy Scripture only in the passage that relates their story. Not so with Noah; both the Old and New Testaments make reference to him; in fact the New Testament writers use him and his times in many typical and practical ways to unfold great truths.

As noted in previous chapters, two Old Testament writers refer directly to the person of Noah, besides the many indirect references made to his times and the flood.

Isaiah's reference is very brief but enlightening. "For this is as the waters of Noah unto me: for as I have sworn that the waters of Noah should no more go over the earth; so have I sworn that I would not be wroth with thee, nor rebuke thee" (Isa 54:9).

This chapter treats of the nation of Israel, chastened and coming out of great tribulation to their inheritance in the millennium; all is future. The main points could be traced out as follows.

1. Fruitfulness in numbers, even after the terrible slaughter of the tribulation (v. 1).
2. The possession of much land, depicted under the figure of a spreading encampment, then a distinct statement, "Thou shalt break forth on the right hand and on the left; and thy seed shall inherit the Gentiles, and

NOAH AND THE PROPHETS

make the desolate cities to be inhabited" (vv. 2-3).

3. The shameful past shall be forgotten, that terrible past of rebellion against God, and the practice of perpetual idolatry. The lean times also shall be forgotten, when Israel dwelt in a state of widowhood, that is, forsaken by God (v. 4).

4. God's renewed relationship with his earthly people, depicted under the figure of husband and wife (vv. 5-6).

5. The two periods that lead to the millennium are then noted: that of the great tribulation, and the consequent restoration (vv. 7-8), Again a beautiful order emerges, the truth is repeated in different forms to assure the hearts of the people. "For a small moment have I forsaken thee" (v. 7a), this is a reference to the great tribulation of Revelation 7."But with great mercies will I gather thee" (v. 7b), is a reference to the future restoration spoken of in Revelation 20.

Both ideas are then repeated in different words. "In a little wrath I hid my face from thee, but with everlasting kindness will I have mercy on thee" (v. 8). The wrath is a direct reference to the tribulation, the mercy being a reference to the restoration.

The grounds of the restoration is the Lord Himself, described in two divine titles: *thy Maker* (v. 5), and *thy Redeemer* (v. 7). Thy Maker suggests the power and wisdom of God, thy Redeemer the grace and love of God.

6. This leads up to the mention of Noah in v. 9. The Lord wants to assure the people of their eternal security. This was necessary because often in the past they had experienced restoration but had drifted back again into idolatry. The restoration here is both different and final. In assuring Israel, the Lord speaks of His faithfulness to His word and promises. Look to the past, the days of Noah for instance. God stated then that He would never

25

NOAH

again judge the whole world by means of water. To give double assurances to Noah and his posterity, God not only spoke, but swore by an oath, "that the waters of Noah would never again cover the earth". Nor has it, nor shall it ever be. He keeps His promises.

In like manner, He has sworn to Israel, "That I would not be wroth with thee, nor rebuke thee", that is, after the final restoration.

The next verse adds to this declaration, "The mountains shall depart, and the hills shall be removed; but my kindness shall not depart from thee". All this is based upon a covenant (v. 9) similar to the covenant made with Noah in Genesis 9. God's covenants always stand firm, so "the waters of Noah" are cited as an example of the faithfulness of God. It is surely wonderful that the Spirit of God makes choice of this example of God's steadfastness, out of the many that appear in the pages of Holy Scripture. The covenant with Noah and the earth shall always stand.

The second Old Testament reference to Noah is found in Ezekiel 14:14, and is more beautiful still. This reference does not take up the waters of the flood as in Isaiah, but rather Noah himself and the lovely character he displayed.

The chapter contains three references to Noah as a person, verses 14, 18, and 20, although in verse 18 he is not mentioned by name as he is in the other two.

Note first that he is coupled with two other great worthies of the Old Testament, Daniel and Job; secondly, righteousness is common to all three; thirdly, they are powerless to deliver the city Jerusalem; and finally, they could deliver only themselves by their accumulated righteousness.

Consider the second point first; this is fundamental.

NOAH AND THE PROPHETS

Here it is by no means a salvation by works as both Daniel and Job confess that they are sinners, and do sin. Listen to Daniel's confession "I prayed unto the Lord and made my confession" (9:14), and again, "We have sinned and committed iniquity and have done wickedly" (v. 5). It is the same with Job, "Behold I am vile" (40:4), and again, "I abhor myself and repent in dust and ashes" (42:6). We must add that Noah manifested the fallen nature in his drunken and naked condition, almost at the close of his life. Nevertheless, all three had faith, "But without faith it is impossible to please him, for he that cometh to God must believe that he is (exists), and that he is a rewarder of them that diligently seek him". (Heb 11:6). The very next verse confirms that Noah had this faith. He knew God, had heard His voice, believed His word and acted in obedience to that word in the building of the ark. So then it was not of works, but he had the actual experience of trusting God and possessing salvation. The same can be said of the other two, as salvation is always on the principle of faith. The outcome is they had righteousness imputed to them on the grounds of that faith; the same is true of all who believe the gospel. David had this experience according to Romans 4:6-8; the same principle is described in Psalm 32:1-2 as is expounded in Romans ch. 4. "Abraham believed God, and it was imputed to him for righteousness" (Gen 15:6). Thus he became the pattern of this wonderful principle and the father of all who believe (Rom 4:16). Abraham then progressed to manifest good works as recorded in Hebrews ch. 11; alas many get very little beyond the initial faith experience. Such should practise righteousness for all to see, a proof that eternal life has been obtained. So the apostle John bears witness. "Ye know that every one that doeth righteousness is born of God" (1 John 2:29). Practical righteousness is therefore essential, but may be present in different degrees, as illustrated in the parable of the sower: some bring forth an hundredfold, some sixty, and some only thirty (Matt13:23). This reference is of course from the viewpoint of the King; He judges from the greatest to the least; see also in the parables of the talents (Matt 25), and of the penny (ch. 20). It is most beautiful to see that in Mark's account, the order is reversed, from the least to the greatest: thirtyfold comes first, then sixty, and finally the hundredfold. The reason for this difference is that Mark is speaking from the viewpoint of a servant, and the Lord expects progress to greater things; besides, even the least service is precious in His sight.

The three men of Ezekiel 14 then where righteous positionally before God, but they also produced the fruit of righteousness to such a degree that God wonderfully acknowledged it. Nevertheless, their rightousness could not have delivered the city but only themselves, had they been in Jerusalem at that time; the governmental judgment of the Lord demanded the doom of the city.

This is the more remarkable when one considers that Daniel was alive when the great statement was made. God remembers the righteous saints of the past, and bears witness to them. He also bears witness to the righteous saints living presently upon earth, and finds great pleasure in them. This is most searching; surely it is something to strive after, that God should be able to witness of us before angels that there are righteous men and women upon the earth.

God bore witness of Job's righteousness while he was still living, addressing Satan with these words, "Hast thou considered my servant Job, that there is none like him in the earth, a perfect and an upright man, one that feareth God, and escheweth evil?" (Job 1:8). Noah is not one iota behind in God's commendation, "Come thou

NOAH AND THE PROPHETS

and all thy house into the ark; for thee have I seen righteous before me in this generation" (Gen 7:21). So all three men had their personal righteousness witnessed to by God while still living.

Note also that all three men had this in common, that a deliverance was experienced through them. Noah was the means of the deliverance of his house, or family (Heb 11:7). He was the channel by which his wife, his sons, and their wives were saved from death by the flood.

Job also was delivered from Satan and all his devices. What an upheaval he experienced in his life, what loss and suffering; and on top of this, to be misunderstood by his closest friends. Out of all this he was delivered, and was the means of the deliverance of his three friends from the consequences of their folly. They behaved very badly towards Job during the time of his trial, and are charged by God with not saying right things about God's dealings. The Lord said to them, "My servant Job shall pray for you: for him I will accept: lest I deal with you after your folly" (Job 42:8); and so the friends were saved from chastisement.

As for Daniel, he was preserved through the upheavals of Jerusalem, and in the courts of Babylon, and was the means of his three friends being delivered from falling to the idolatrous wiles of Nebuchadnezzar (Dan 1). Again, he prophesied about the deliverance Jerusalem would experience in a coming day (Dan 9).

So all three were used to deliver others, Noah and his family, Daniel and his companions, and Job and his friends.

But the context in which these names appear in Ezekiel 14 is most solemn. Because of sin Jerusalem had been besieged and a number were taken prisoner, Ezekiel and the elders of Jerusalem among them. They are in a

NOAH

prisoner of war camp by the river Cheber, and the news from Jerusalem is not good. The city is under king Zedekiah, a worthless man, the former king having been carried away into captivity by Nebuchadnezzar in a sort of punitive raid. The people imprisoned by the river, are looking forward to being released, and to being able to return to their beloved city. In fact, some false prophets are saying just this, supposedly from the Lord. Ezekiel is the damper; he keeps prophesying of the city in ruins, and its temple being destroyed. The elders have appeared before him, perhaps to reason with him about these things, or to hear the latest prophecy. In themselves, they think they are blameless, that the sins of their forefathers are the reason for their present distress. Outwardly they look quite religious and God fearing. "But the Lord looks upon the heart" and sees all the idolatry hidden there. In verses 3,4, 5, and 7 the same formula occurs, "Idols in their hearts", and the repetition manifests how serious it is in the sight of God. Deliverance is out of the question, and not in God's plans.

What a message this turned out to be to the self righteous elders, who were of the opinion that God was obliged to deliver them because they were righteous. To such arrogance, the Lord presents His case: if righteous Noah, Daniel, and Job were in the city, they would be able to deliver only themselves; they could not affect the deliverance of others, although; they had been the means of doing so in the past. The city Jerusalem had gone too far; judgment was pending, and the only deliverance would be individual, as one felt his sin, and turned in obedience to God.

The world is in the same condition today; nothing can hold back the coming judgment upon this Christ rejecting scene, in which God is displaced by anything

NOAH AND THE PROPHETS

and everything. Yet God in grace through the gospel message offers salvation to the individual on the principle of faith. Few respond to it, but those who do embrace Christ are delivered from the coming storms of wrath (1 Thess 1:10). This fact is made clear throughout Scripture, that salvation is an individual matter; no man can by any means redeem his brother; every man must believe for himself, is the message that Peter preached on the day of Pentecost, "Save yourselves from this untoward or crooked generation" (Acts 2:40). Alas today few enter in through the opened door (Luke 13:23-24).

But more serious still, many believers are following afar off, and idols of some sort are cherished in the heart although outwardly all seems to be well. We live in a covetous world, and covetousness is idolatry (Col 3:5). The Lord often warned of the danger of covetousness; Luke 12:13-21 is a good example of this. There, a man was warned of the danger of covetousness who was seeking to obtain what he thought was rightly his. To him the Lord spoke the parable of the "Rich Fool". It was not a case of coveting what others had, but of selfishly holding on to what he possessed, and not dispersing his abundance to those that were needy. There is always the danger of *things* shutting out God, and if man does this, then really he has nothing.

Returning to Ezekiel 14, and those three righteous men, a little distinction is seen in that Noah overcame the world that then was, Daniel overcame the flesh in refusing the king's meat and wine, and Job overcame the devil. So the threefold enemy of the child of God was clearly overcome in these three righteous men.

Finally, Noah is named first in each reference, not because he appears the first in the Bible record, but rather because he was the means of delivering his family. Verse 20 makes this point clear, "They shall deliver neither son nor daughter", indicating that if Noah could not do so in the present Jerusalem circumstances, much less the elders or any man of Israel at that time.

Thus, we have examined the Old Testament references to Noah: the character of Noah in Ezekiel ch. 14, and the flood bearing witness to the faithfulness of God's word and oath in Isaiah chap 54 to give assurance to Israel. Now these are opposites: Ezekiel would say, "Look at Noah, there is no hope for Israel, judgment is sure. Even Noah could not produce a means of deliverance for the Israel of this day". Howbeit, the Israel to come *will be* delivered and restored. God will restore them for ever, for God is faithful to all His covenants as He has been to His covenant with Noah since the flood (Isa 54:9).

4

NOAH IN MATTHEW'S GOSPEL.

When an Old Testament character is referred to in passages of the Bible other than that which records his actual history, then he is a character of some importance; God has great lessons there. When the individual is referred to many times in the New Testament, then he must be of considerable importance. Noah is such a case. Let us consider that the first person to make reference to Noah was our Lord Himself in the Gospels, and He did so in Matthew 24:37-9, and the parallel passage in Luke 17:26-7.

The comparison our Lord makes between Noah's day and the days preceeding His coming, is often emphasised by gospel preachers and teachers. In doing so, they generally present a parallel between the violence and corruption of that past day and the present days, and conclude that the coming of the Lord is very near. However, nothing is said in Matthew 24 and Luke 17 about the violent and sinful condition of the people; it was rather the carelessness and wilful ignorance that prevailed in those days. Life went on as normal in spite of signs of divine movements. The world is never aware of, or ready for the judgment of God.

In the discourse the Lord tells us nothing at all about Noah: there is no mention of what kind of man he was, nor of his work in building the ark, nor of his righteousness. In fact, if we seek information about the man personally, the Gospel references are not the places to look. What the Lord does speak of, and presses home is, the careless attitude of the people in Noah's time, those dreadful days. The Lord compares the people then, and those of Sodom and Gomorrah in Lot's time (Luke 17:28), with those that shall live in the days prior to the Coming of the Son of man. The attitude of the people is the same: careless, unable to discern the times, and ignorant of the impending doom soon to come upon them.

This present time is similar to Noah's day: the worldling gives little heed to the claims of God in His Word, nor to the practice of righteousness, nor to the momentous events that are swiftly heading up to the end. No wonder the Book of Revelation continually refers to the masses as "earth-dwellers"; all they live for is time, and this earth. Even the rapture of the church will fail to alter the attitude of the world at large.

Let us consider in a little detail the words of our Lord concerning the people amongst whom Noah lived. It will be profitable to consider first the context of the passages to get the thrust of the Lord's warning, then it will be easy to gather what the Lord actually said about the times and character of the people.

In Matthew 24 the reference to Noah falls almost in the centre of the great Olivet discourse, one of the great prophetic outlines in Scripture. Like the parables in Matthew 13, it contains things new and old. One useful feature of the Olivet discourse is that the Lord sets forth the events in a chronological sequence. The Book of Revelation is not so; it is rather set out in subjects, and this confuses many. Some events in later chapters take place before those in earlier chapters. A good example of this occurs in chs. 13 and 17; the ten horns are not crowned in ch. 17, but are in ch. 13, so ch. 17 actually precedes ch. 13 chronologically. Matthew chs. 24-5 is a

NOAH IN MATTHEW'S GOSPEL

great chronological table by which to set the order of events in the last days; this helps to clear up many difficult passages elsewhere in the prophetic Scriptures.

Now in the discourse, the Lord carries forward His prophetic unfolding up to "the return of the Son of man in power and great glory" (24:31). He then pauses to apply certain lessons. The Lord always applied His ministry, it is something one should emulate; not every minister of the Word or Bible teacher is skilful in this respect. The great lesson the Lord would impress upon the four original disciples who were present at the discourse (Mark 13:3), and to all who read is, "Watch, for ye know not the hour". The teaching was calculated to create an attitude of watchfulness. To secure this the Lord used three devices: firstly, parables of which there are five; then assurances, the certainty of the event; and finally parallels, references to the fate of the careless, non watching people in the times of Noah.

Note the order.

1. Parable, The fig tree (v. 32).
2. Assurance, "this generation shall not pass away until all is fulfilled" (v. 34).
3. Assurance, "Heaven and earth shall pass away, my word shall never pass away" (v. 35).
4. Parallel, "The days of Noah" (vv. 36-41).
5. Parable, The goodman of the house (v. 43).
6. Parable, The wise and unwise servants (v. 45).
7. Parable, The wise, and foolish virgins (25:1-14).
8. Parable, The talents and the servants (25:15-30).

After this practical application, the Lord continues with the prophecy from ch. 25:31, now making reference to the judgment upon the earth at His coming, as previously taught in ch. 24:30-31. Considering this, all

35

that lies between ch. 24:31 and ch. 25:31 is a parenthesis, being the application of the lesson, "Watch Therefore". The elect in the earlier passage are Israel, then the nations are dealt with in ch. 25, the sheep and the goats, and all go into the kingdom.

Note the constant warnings dispersed throughout this section. "Watch therefore ye know not what hour your Lord doth come" (v. 42).

"If the goodman of the house had known what watch the thief would come, he would have watched" (v. 43).

"My Lord delayeth his coming...and shall begin to smite his fellow servants, and to eat and drink with the drunken. The lord of that servant shall come in a day when he looketh not for him" (v.48ff).

"Watch therefore, for ye know neither the day nor the hour wherein the Son of man cometh" (25:13).

In particular note the warning of ch. 24:44, "Therefore be ye also ready: for in such an hour as ye think not the Son of man cometh".

So Noah is cited as an example, or rather a warning not to be part of a careless non-watching generation, a generation that fails to discern the times. The world is never ready for the judgment of God, the generation that lived before the flood is typical of all such. They were not aware of any danger, and this resulted in a total lack of repentance.

It would be fitting here to use the closing statement of Mark's version of the Olivet discourse: "What I say unto you, I say unto all, Watch" (13:37). Mark does not refer to the days of Noah, but records the key thought in the discourse. Matthew, being the dispensational Gospel, after the warnings to watch, proceeds to speak of the judgment of the nations, and the setting up of the kingdom (ch.25). The story of the sheep and the goats is not a parable but a fact, an event, namely the judgment of the living nations at the Lord's return, and the Lord uses metaphoric language to distinguish the character of the saved and the unsaved.

It would be good if ministering brethren speaking on prophecy would endeavour to produce in the hearers an attitude of watchfulness, and not seek only to satisfy the curious minds of the people: "The coming of the Lord draweth nigh" (James 5:8).

5

NOAH IN LUKE'S GOSPEL

The Gospel of Luke is not dispensational as is Matthew's, rather is it moral; it is to do with priests and temples. Devotion, love, joy and worship are its main themes. Nevertheless there are references to the future, and in ch. 17 is one of them. Noah and his days are alluded to there in a different setting altogether from Matthew.

In Matthew ch. 24-5 the Lord has already suffered rejection by Israel and is awaiting the deadly onslaught of the enemy. From that standpoint He gives the great prophetic outline of the future of Israel. In Luke ch. 17:20 the Lord is approached by the Pharisees demanding "when the kingdom of God should come". Seemingly they had fixed ideas of coming events, and trusted in the teaching of their Rabbis. What the Lord taught seemed to be contrary to the way they looked at things. Really they were blind to the wonderful movements of God, and the Lord often accused them of being so. The religious leaders could not see that the King was already in the midst of the people (v. 21). John the Baptist had said the same, "There standeth one among you, (or in the midst of you), whom ye know not" (John 1:26). Perhaps they had an excuse then as the Lord had not yet revealed Himself; but now, in Luke ch. 17, many miracles and proofs of His Messiahship had been accomplished. Many words of grace had been uttered by the Man of whom the people said, "Never man spake like this man". The evidence was there; the King was present; they were

NOAH IN LUKE'S GOSPEL

without excuse; the kingdom had come. The Lord follows this encounter with a short discourse to His disciples on His two comings: His present one in grace, and that which was to follow in power and glory, the coming which is the subject of the Olivet discourse. The passage in vv. 22-30 may seem to be quite difficult until one realises that the Lord is speaking about two different advents.

Note the references to the Son of man.

1. One of the days of the Son of man (v. 22).
2. The Son of man in His day (v. 24).
3. In the days of the Son of man (v. 26).
4. When the Son of man is revealed (v. 30).

Here is an example of a numeric principle in Scripture, that a four is often divided into a three and a one. The reference in v. 22 is to the first advent of our Lord, the other three are to the second advent.

Luke's purpose is not to expound either advent, but to show that neither advent comes with a great noise or fuss, God quietly brings the events to pass, although signs may precede each coming as the Gospels plainly teach. Luke makes a distinction between various persons' attitudes to these events. What stumbled the religious leaders and the Pharisees concerning the first coming of our Lord in grace, was their wrong conception of the prophetic writings. They were looking for all to be glorious, and had no thought of humility and suffering. Those with understanding were not stumbled; accordingly Simeon and Anna accept the babe, and speak to others of His humility, suffering and redemption (Luke ch. 2).

With reference to the second advent, Luke joins with Matthew in identifying carelessness, a lack of watching, as being the stumbling block in the last days. To press home this fact, both refer to the days of Noah. So, here is a section that enlarges upon the fact that a false sense of peace prevails when there is no peace. A careless attitude shall characterise the people prior to the coming of the Lord in glory. To further emphasise this, Luke adds the days of Lot in Sodom to the days of Noah. In both cases the people were unaware of divine movements in judgment, as people in this day are largely unaware of the visitation of grace in the gospel being preached. (vv. 21-22).

To sum up, Matthew 24 is prophetical, and Noah and the parables are introduced to reinforce an exhortation to watchfulness. On the other hand Luke is teaching that people are unaware of God's times and movements, and are therefore careless. This attitude is described very succinctly by Paul in 1 Thess 5:2, and by Peter in 2 Peter 3:10; both writers use the phrase "as a thief in the night". The Lord Himself was the originator of this fitting illustration; He used it in Luke 12:39, and again in Matthew 24:43.

So then, Noah is cited in Matthew in a warning to watch, speaking to the generation that will see the return of the Lord. In Luke the Lord uses Noah to condemn his own generation for failing to recognise him at His first coming. The world at large is ignorant of divine visitations whether in grace or in judgment, an evil that seems to persist continually in the heart of man.

Let us return briefly to Matthew 24, and to the actual words of our Lord concerning Noah: "But as the days of Noah were" (v. 37), and, "For as in the days that were before the flood". Many are of the opinion that in comparing the days of Noah and the days before the coming of the Son of man, the parallel is in the stage of corruption and violence reached in each time. So that unprecedented corruption and violence is a sign that judgment is near. This is not the point; the people were unaware of any signs that may have been given by God; rather it is the careless ways of the people with which He is seeking to occupy the hearer, and not the dreadful sin of the people, awful as that was. Nor is there any reference to Noah himself. The Lord gives no information about the man, nor his preaching, nor his faith, nor anything other than his entering into the ark. The lesson is, "Do not be careless like that generation who perished because they did not discern the times".

The Lord is not speaking of years before the flood, but rather of the days immediately preceeding that great deluge. Note verse 38, "For as in the days that were before the flood they were eating and drinking, marrying and giving in marriage until *the day* that Noah entered into the ark". Although there were many indications that something unusual was about to happen, that generation did not perceive them. No doubt the reason was that there was much to occupy, both in pleasure and in the social life, eating, drinking and marrying. Again, note that there is no mention of work and labour. Of the days of Lot it is said, "they planted, they builded". The generation of Noah seems to have been pleasure-seeking to the exclusion of all else. The appetites of the flesh were much in evidence, which in turn made them blind and careless to the times and their dreadful outcome. Nothing seemed to disturb the sleep of carelessness.

Noah laid the framework of the ark; perhaps some were amused, but they ate and drank. Noah preached righteousness (2 Pet 2:5), they continued to eat and drink. The ark is now almost complete, they take no notice; still they feast and are merry in marriage. At last the ark is finished, the last plank is in place, the last nail driven home; still the social, pleasurable life continues.

41

NOAH

Noah begins to gather food, to stockpile the provision, and animals come to him; the people take no notice. Still they are gripped by the appetites of the natural man. They ate and drank right up to the day that Noah entered into the ark. The Genesis record informs that the Lord called him into the ark, and the door was shut. This eating and drinking was not the fatalistic idea of 1 Cor 15:32, "Let us eat and drink for tomorrow we die". Noah's generation felt no danger, nor did they realise how soon death would overtake them, nor that the pleasurable things in which they were engaged were being enjoyed for the last time. The whole scene is like the parable in Luke 12 concerning a prosperous man bent on pleasure, and thinking he had many years left to indulge himself. Yet he died that night. The people of Noah's day were fools, they had reckoned without God, and were asleep as to their awful doom. Things were happening, and something unforeseen was about to happen, they could not discern the times (Luke 12:56). If only they had considered the increasing corruption and violence, they would have reasoned that a judgment was bound to come; that things just could not continue as they were; that sowing is always followed by reaping.

Is not the same condition with us today? Now is our salvation nearer than when we believed (Rom 13:11), and the world is hurtling on to judgment. The world today witnesses violence and corruption on a scale far beyond the days of Noah, and added to this is the awful falsehood that is abounding amidst all nations everywhere. How careless are the people of this day. The lust for power is in all circles; covetousness and pleasures fill the heart of the average man and woman of this generation The preaching of the gospel goes largely unheeded, the Bible is seldom read even by Christians, and on many sides it is discredited. The days of Noah are

NOAH IN LUKE'S GOSPEL

with us again; increasingly it will be so, until the coming of the Son of man.

One significant point must not be passed over: they ate and drank "until the day that Noah entered into the ark". It does not say until the flood came, but until the day that Noah disappeared from sight! Does this suggest a shock? Noah is gone, he cannot be seen; the eating and drinking would seem less important then. The Christians today wait for His Son from heaven (1 Thess 1:9-10); they all shall disappear at the rapture of the church as described in 1 Thess 4:13-18. A door was opened in heaven to John (Rev 4:1), a fitting illustration of our passing beyond the veil of heaven, and out of the sight of this world. Those left behind will no doubt experience a shock, but as in Noah's day they will soon recover from it, "they knew not until the flood came" (Matt 24:39). Then they knew, but it was too late.

We must remember that the preaching of Noah was not a warning about a coming flood, nor was it an invitation to come into the ark, but a call to repentance, a call to turn away from the corruption and violence. He preached righteousness; had the people hearkened as the men of Ninevah did under the preaching of Jonah, who knows but that the judgment may have been averted and the old world spared.

It came as a shock to that careless generation when Noah entered into the ark; but they soon recovered. The blindness continued another seven days, then came another terrible shock: the flood.

The Lord adds a solemn postscript to this: "The flood came and took them all away". There was a separation: Noah to life in the ark, the others to the judgment of the flood. Even so a separation shall take place at the return of the Lord. Two shall be in a field, one taken, the other left. Two women shall be grinding at the mill, the one

NOAH

taken, the other left. How sudden and eternal this separation; people, neighbours, even some of the same family in the same house, shall be eternally separated. The Lord uttered solemn words in Luke 12:52. "There shall be five in one house divided, three against two, and two against three". While the words no doubt refer to the great tribulation times, yet they are always true. The first household in Scripture was divided: Abel was blessed of the Lord; Cain his brother was of the wicked one, and was cursed (1 John 3:12).

Again, it is searching to see that none escaped: the flood came and took them *all* away; not one survived as the record in Genesis makes very clear. "The end of all flesh is come before me" (Gen 6:13). Again, "and all flesh died that moved upon the earth" (7:21). Again, "every living substance was destroyed which was upon the face of the ground" (7:23). The words "took them all away" are echoed in Paul's teaching in Romans 2:3, concerning the judgment of God. "Thinkest thou this O man... that thou shalt escape the judgment of God?" The same idea occurs again in 1 Thess 5:3: "then sudden destruction cometh upon them, as travail upon a woman with child; and they shall not escape".

It is most important to draw attention to the title "the Son of man", and how it is used. In Matthew the Lord calls the time before Noah entered into the ark "the days before the flood", and links these with the days before the coming of the Son of man, that is with, the great prophetic "day of the Lord". In Luke He uses the title differently, "And as it was in the days of Noe, so shall it be also in the days of the Son of man" (Luke 17:26). What does the Lord mean by the strange phrase, "the *days* of the Son of man?.

Some light can perhaps be obtained by considering Paul's use of a similar term in 1 Cor 4:3: "With me it is a small thing that I should be judged of you, or of man's judgment". The last phrase would be better rendered "man's day", as in Darby's New Translation, and in the margin of the RV. This is man's day: the natural man judges and does as he likes; God seemingly keeps silent. It is a principle with God to let evil develop, and today man seems to have a very long rope; he can do what he likes without any recompense, even to the persecution of the people of God. Trace the persecutions under imperial Rome in the apostolic days: the banishing of the old man John; Polycarp burned to death in a most horrible way; the days of the fires of Smithfield and the burning of the martyrs. All this surely indicates that this is "man's day". Certainly "the most high ruleth in the kingdoms of men", and man eventually reaps what he sows; yet the fact remains, man seemingly is uncontrollable, without the fear of God, and persisting in his own will. We live in man's day, but this state of affairs shall not continue. The days of the Son of man that immediately precede His coming will see the Lord taking control. Man shall follow a pattern, the blueprint of heaven, all issuing from the throne of Revelation chapter 4-7. Then man shall not do as he will, all will be predetermined by God. The opened seals, and the judgments of the trumpets and bowls (Rev chs. 6-16) demonstrate that man will meet just retribution for all his behaviour. Man's day will continue until the rapture of the church, then the Son of man will intervene. The days that follow are called "the days of the Son of man". These things which must shortly come to pass John saw from the viewpoint of heaven; all issues from that glorious throne of Rev chapter 4.

An entirely different idea is in mind in verse 22. "The days will come, when ye shall desire to see one of the days of the Son of man, and ye shall not see it". Here the

NOAH

Lord was referring to His ministry during the days of His flesh. The Lord was there in grace; such blessing and truth were dispensed on every hand. In tribulation days people shall desire a day just like that, but no such day shall be; all shall be tribulation, and judgment. The two comings of the Lord Jesus are very distinct: grace and judgment.

A further difference is to be noted in the Luke account: the reference to the days of Lot. To the eating and drinking of Noah's day is added the industry of the days of Lot: they bought, they sold, they planted, they builded, up until the time the fire and brimstone fell from heaven and destroyed them all in the cities of the plain (Luke 17:28-9). At least, industry was there which is not mentioned of the days of Noah. But Luke has an aversion to covetousness and the desire for the possessions of this world. He often approaches a subject with this in mind, and so differently from the other Gospels. He is always seeking to give a lesson on the dangers and snares of covetousness. Consider the parable of chapter 12; the background is, "Take heed, and beware of covetousness: for a man's life consisteth not in the abundance of the things which he possesseth" (Luke 12:15). This warning was directed to a man who wanted his brother to divide an earthly inheritance with him. The subject of the parable is similar to that of the Sermon on the Mount (Matt 6:25-34): anxiety about material things. And yet they look in opposite directions. Whereas Matthew focusses on the anxiety of not having enough to survive, Luke warns against the folly of striving to provide for a day we may not live to see. In Matthew the teaching is, Trust in the Lord to supply the need; but in Luke it is, trusting in self to hold onto what they have, and to accumulate more, in other words, covetousness.

So in the days of Lot, possessions and gain are to the

fore, and Luke alone in keeping with the tenor of his Gospel records that point.

Such then is the description by our Lord of the careless people before the flood, and the comparison of a like attitude before His return. May all who read examine the world today; this attitude is rife; it can be observed on every hand. We ought to examine ourselves to see if carelessness or covetousness marks us. Let us look for our Lord's return, and occupy in His service until He comes.

6

NOAH IN HEBREWS CHAPTER 11

As usual, our Lord leads the way; others follow. The Lord has presented a great lesson from the times of Noah as already traced in the Gospels. Two New Testament writers likewise draw profitable truths from the subject. However, it is Noah himself rather than his times, that the epistle writers examine.

Hebrews chapter 11 contains the first of these references, and in that magnificent passage Noah is placed among the great examples of faith. In fact, in one aspect he shines beyond the other worthies mentioned there. Although only one verse is devoted to his presentation, yet that verse begins and ends with the word "faith". Each character in the chapter is introduced by the formula "by faith", but the record of Noah has the peculiarity of ending in the way it begins (v. 7).

The verse is as follows. "By faith Noah, being warned of God of things not seen as yet, moved with fear, prepared an ark to the saving of his house; by the which he condemned the world, and became heir of the righteousness which is by faith".

A careful reader of the text will quickly appreciate that the writer approaches the historic Noah in an entirely different way from that of our Lord. In the Gospel record the Lord drew lessons from the times in which Noah lived, and emphasised the careless people who could not discern the times. The Lord made no reference whatever to Noah personally. Howbeit, this single verse

NOAH IN HEBREWS CHAPTER 11

in Hebrews does the reverse, presenting Noah himself, his exercise, and work, and making no reference to the people of that day, except to point out their condemnation.

In all, seven things are brought out by the inspired writer concerning Noah personally.

1. By faith Noah — He was a man of faith.
2. Being warned of God — He was favoured by God.
3. Moved with fear — He was a convicted man.
4. Prepared an ark — A man of action.
5. To the saving of his house — His family, wife, sons, and their wives.
6. Condemned the world — Left all without excuse.
7. Became the heir of righteousness — Entered into blessing.

The work of preparing the ark justified the reality of his faith (see James 2). The saving of his house included himself: eight people in all.

The seven points of information fall into the usual pattern of a four and a three, which is general in Scripture with the number seven. The first four are the *facts*, and the last three are the *effects*, being the outcome of the first four.

Note how all hinges on the exercise of faith, which manifests itself in the fear of the warning of God. Faith takes the word of God seriously. Noah believed the warning and prepared the ark. The prepared ark standing there, and no sign of floods or rain as yet, was the evidence of his faith. The prepared ark lead to the saving of his household, the condemning of the world, and the becoming heir of the righteousness.

Noah then is one of the great examples of faith in the Bible, one from whom God demonstrates principles that are binding upon all that believe, and for all time.

1. works are the evidence of the possessed faith.
2. faith comes by hearing the word of God. Faith can rest only upon what God has spoken.
3. Righteousness is imputed only to those who believe.

As to the first, Paul sums up this principle in the words of "your work of faith" (1 Thess 1:3). The Jews to whom the Hebrew epistle is addressed, made the mistake of clinging to dead works (9:14). Dead works are works perhaps good in themselves, but produced by law and ritual rather than by faith. These dead works are different from the evil works that the ungodly produce as living without God, and are different of course from the good works that the believer produces by faith and the Spirit of God. Judaism and all its ritual still entangled some of the true believers. These are dead works, says the writer, You must leave the camp and go out to the unseen Jesus. Faith introduces God, and when God is there, life is bound to be manifested in some way.

The seven statements fall into an interesting pattern, that of inverted parallels as follows.

A. By faith Noah, principle--------Received the warning.
 B. Warned of God----------------Warning heeded.
  C. Moved by fear----------------Sorrow, conviction.
   D. Prepared an ark--------------The central movement.
  C. Saving of house-------------- Joy and salvation
 B. Condemned the world-------- Warning unheeded
A. By faith, principle----------------Received righteousness.

The prominent note is faith, beginning and ending the series. The centre piece is the building of the ark, being the obedience of faith as emphasised in the case of Abraham: "By faith Abraham when he was called... obeyed" (v. 8). Paul's commission was to produce the obedience of faith among all nations (Rom 1:5). As can be seen from the stated parallels each is duplicated except the centre one. The prepared ark looks back over the first three statements, and is the outcome of hearing the warning of God, believing it and being moved by it. The last three statements look forward, and are the outcome of the prepared ark in the threefold way already considered. These seven virtues will be examined in the next chapter.

7

THE SEVEN POINTS OF NOAH'S FAITH

"By faith Noah, being warned of God of things not seen as yet, moved with fear, prepared an ark to the saving of his house; by which he condemned the world, and became heir of the righteousness which is by faith" (Heb 11:7).

As pointed out in the former chapter, there are seven statements in this verse all linked in some way to the faith of Noah. A closer look at these will enrich the inquirer.

The verse commences "by faith Noah", but faith is qualified; it can only be exercised when God speaks: "faith cometh by hearing, and hearing by the word of God" (Rom 10:17). So God must have spoken in some way to Noah, and the Genesis record tells that the Lord did just that: "The end of all flesh is come before me... make thee an ark of gopher wood" (Gen 6:13ff). This message Noah believed no matter how impossible it seemed.

Later the same principle was seen in Abraham. God said to the old and childless man, "Look at the stars, so shall thy seed be". Abraham did not question the word; it seemed impossible to the natural man, but the man of faith received it. He believed God. He did not doubt nor reason nor laugh as did Sarah when confronted with the same promise. To Abraham, God was able to perform what He promised, and he believed, and it was accounted unto him for righteousness.

Noah no doubt pressed home in his preaching that destruction was coming. That was the word of God through Noah, yet the people did not believe. In the

THE SEVEN POINTS OF NOAH'S FAITH

preaching of the gospel man is faced with but two alternatives: believe the message, or refuse it; which of course means that there are only two classes of people. So in Luke 13:24-5 the Lord spoke of two gates only, of two roads, and of two destinies. If only people would realise this! They constantly think there is middle ground. In the days of Noah all that were inside the ark were saved, all that were outside perished. In Exodus 16 the Lord tested the people with the manna: the obedience in gathering this, or the lack of it, divided the people into two classes. The Lord said, "Whether they will walk in my law or no" (Ex 16:4). So today, not by manna, but by the One of whom the manna speaks, God is testing and dividing mankind. The gospel is a savour unto life or unto death; there must be faith in Christ. All this could be called *the principle of faith*.

Secondly we have *the grounds of his faith:* "being warned of God of things not seen as yet". There was no evidence other than God's word. God spoke to him and he believed; he was standing on good ground.

The phrase "things not seen as yet" is similar to that at the end of verse 1: "Now faith is the substance of things hoped for, the evidence of things not seen". Noah had never seen a flood, nor a world wide judgment of God; some suggest that he had never even seen rain, for until that time rain was unknown; the earth was watered as in Genesis 2:5-6: "there went up a mist from the earth, and watered the whole face of the ground". Yet Noah believed, and the proof of that was seen in his "being moved by fear". No doubt he placed the same evidence of the word before the people in his preaching, but they did not believe. Thus the faith defined in verse one is identified in Noah in verse seven.

God spoke to Noah about the judgment; he had only a word; he had no tangible evidence, nor had he seen a

NOAH

vision, or anything like a vision; he had only the word. He believed, so he was afraid: God cannot lie. He saw everything so clearly although as yet there was nothing. He was convicted that all would be just as the Lord had said. It was true of him as of Abraham that he staggered not at the magnitude of the Word of God; rather he was fully persuaded that what God had promised he was able, and would fully perform. "Blessed are they that have not seen, and yet have believed" (John 20:29).

This lead to *the conviction of faith*: "moved by fear". The phrase has been dealt with already. Suffice it to say that there was a response in his heart to the word of God. The fear of God is the beginning of wisdom; therefore the worldly wise who fear not God are not wise at all.

God looks for a response where-ever and whenever His word is read and explained to either saved or unsaved. If there is no response to it, then there can be no blessing from it. Fear, thanksgiving, faith and love are all attitudes that can emerge in response to the word of God.

We come now to the central statement on which all the rest hinge: "prepared an ark". Here is *the proof of faith*. His faith is now demonstrated by action; he acted swiftly upon what he had heard and believed: faith without works is dead (James 2:26).

James is very searching in his little epistle. He also makes reference to Abraham as a proof that genuine faith is always manifested in some way. With Abraham it was the obedience of faith agreeing with Hebrews 11:8. If Noah had said that he believed and yet had failed to build the ark, it would have been evident that he had not believed at all. Thus there would have been no deliverance from the flood. He would have perished with the rest apart from the ark. Who of his generation

THE SEVEN POINTS OF NOAH'S FAITH

would have said that Noah believed if no ark had been a-building? if the people would have known that he did not really believe, how much more God? who looks for the evidence of the faith that He knows exists.

How suitable all this was to the Hebrew believers. They said that they had believed, but they were not going on. Rather in heart some were going back to the Judaism they had already left. Was their faith real? The whole epistle was written to encourage them to manifest the reality of their faith by going on, and going outside the camp of Judaism.

So the ark was the evidence that Noah had really believed, and that his belief was firmly and entirely based upon the word of God.

In the fifth statement, "to the saving of his house", we have *the salvation of* faith. His house was of course his family, which in this case consisted of his wife, his three sons, and their three wives: seven in all that he was the means of saving. No mention is made of the many animals that were saved, yet so much is made of this by those that read. The animals were necessary to replenish the earth (Gen 8:17). God has His chief interest in people, those who have a living soul and a conscience, who, if they come to possess salvation, can commune with Him. The conscience can be reached, the soul and spirit of man can be saved, and both can develop to the glory of God. This is not so with the animals.

Animals are clever and possess great instincts; they can be trained to do wonderful things, but they cannot know or value divine things. How different are humans: they have a God-breathed spirit within, and the first man was made in the image and likeness of God. Man is still in the image of God; the likeness was lost in the fall; that was the moral likeness to God, but the image is still retained. So in this reference to Noah, the salvation of humans is taken note of and not the saving of animals from the destruction of the flood. In fact no other reference makes mention of the animals apart from Genesis chapters 6-9.

We shall call the second outcome, *the witness of faith*: "he condemned the world". In what sense did he condemn the world? Could it be a reference to his preaching? No doubt that preaching left them without excuse, but the preaching is not referred to in the verse. Could it be the flood that condemned? Surely they knew their sinful condition and God's just anger with them when the flood came and took they all away. Then for an awful moment they saw that Noah was right; they likely remembered his preaching and realised they were condemned to a judgment they deserved.

It would seem rather that the *ark in building* was the condemnation of the then world. The phrase "prepared an ark" is central, and this condemnation is noticeable as being one of the three results that issued from that central statement. This condemned the people long before the flood came, and perhaps even a great while before he started to preach. The boat taking shape was a loud voice: God was speaking. Each plank of wood put in place and each nail driven home was adding to the condemnation of the careless people. Noah was different in manner of life from what they were; he professed to know God. They ought to have known that the constructing of an ark meant something. Why was there no inquiry, no repentance? Alas the careless people were condemned already (John 3:36).

The sons are not mentioned as helping in any way; maybe they did, but not a Scripture anywhere even suggests the idea. Noah himself seems to have done all the building; it was his faith, work and labour that produced the finished ark. In doing so he personally was

THE SEVEN POINTS OF NOAH'S FAITH

the channel in saving his family and condemning the world. How like our Lord Jesus he was, who Himself alone provided salvation in the great work of Calvary, and condemns all those who refuse to repent. 1 Peter 3:10 supports all this, "The long suffering of God waited in the days of Noah while the ark was a preparing". The warning had been clear and long; when the flood came all were righteously judged. Noah as a carpenter condemned the world.

Faith's reward was that he "became heir of the righteousness which is by faith".

He inherited a new world. All was so different after the flood, and a divine covenant was established with him. The new world was very prosperous, and is believed by many prophetic students to have been a picture of the coming millennium. Wonderful as this was, it was not the prize spoken of here. The righteousness by faith is the same as that of Abraham (Gen 15:6), the righteousness of God imputed on the principle of faith and not works, as so ably expounded by Paul in Romans chapters 3-4.

Noah of course is included in verse 13: "These all died in faith, not having received the promises, but having seen them afar off, and were persuaded of them, and embraced them, and confessed that they were strangers and pilgrims on the earth". Verse 16 adds that God recognises all such; He has prepared for them a city, a heavenly city. Noah had not his sights set upon the old earth before the flood, nor on that which followed after the flood, blessed as the new world was. Rather he looked for something eternal, perfect, spiritual, an enduring substance, and he became heir to all that by faith.

So faith brought him safely through the flood and into the new creation of God. He worked more than any man of his time: he built the ark unassisted, a mammoth task, but he did not lean upon this, nor any other work, for the next life. Rather faith, confidence in what God had said, was the ground of all his blessings, the only principle that God will acknowledge.

All that is written of Abraham in Romans chapter 4 could well be said about Noah also. The promise that he should experience deliverance and be carried through to a new order of things was not by the law of works, but by the righteousness of faith (Rom 4:13). Noah indeed, "against hope believed in God" (v. 18). He was not weak in faith (v. 19). He staggered not at the promise of God through unbelief, but was strong in faith giving God the glory (v. 20).

Noah would have been swift to say that all his blessings stemmed from that warning from God. He believed, and it was accounted unto him for righteousness.

How wonderful that all believers in our Lord Jesus are blessed on that same principle, and are added to that illustrious company of Hebrews chapter 11. Again as in Noah's experience, God has moved towards mankind in the person of His Son, who has spoken of the great salvation amid solemn warnings (Heb 2:1-4). All that believe the gospel, the statements that God has made concerning the Person and work of His Son, are blessed for ever more. Such believers are also made heirs of the righteousness which is by faith, and are now found in Christ, and fitted for the presence of God eternally. Such is the assurance of Romans 4:24-5: righteousness is imputed to us also, "if we believe on him that raised up Jesus our Lord from the dead".

Such wonderful statements God has made of His Son, and of all who trust in Him; these are living waters to thirsty souls.

So the writer of Hebrews ch. 11 presents Noah the

THE SEVEN POINTS OF NOAH'S FAITH

man, and such a man. Yet all the grace of God is there: he was a man that feared God and believed in God, a man of action seen in the preparation of the ark. He was a blessing to his family, a warning to all his neighbours, and an heir of all the blessings of God. Faith is all.

A final summing up of the verse appears as follows.

By faith Noah ----------------- The principle of faith.
Being warned of God ------- The grounds of faith.
Moved with fear -------------- The conviction of faith.
Prepared an ark -------------- The proof of faith.
The saving of family --------- The salvation by faith.
Condemned the world ------ The witness of faith.
Became heir ------------------- The reward of faith.

8

REFERENCES TO NOAH IN 1 PETER

Peter, that great apostle and successful gospel preacher, appears to be a very versatile man, and quite a keen student of Scripture as well. Some parts of his epistles are as deep as any.

Like most serious students of the word of God, he specialised upon certain themes and sections of the Book of God. For instance, his exceptional understanding of the Psalms is evident in his sermons in the book of Acts, and his two epistles abound with references to the Psalms.

Noah, and his times is another subject that attracted his attention in a special way; in both his epistles he makes references to this subject far beyond any other Scripture, with the exception of Genesis itself. In fact, most of his "hard to be understood" passages deal with Noah and the events connected with him.

However, his approach to the whole subject is very different from that of the Lord and the writer of Hebrews. Whereas they speak of the *times* and of *Noah himself* respectively, Peter rather takes the same subject and gives a wonderful exposition of *God Himself*: he uses Noah as a platform to declare the character and ways of God that were magnificently displayed. He seemingly carefully studied the record of the flood, and saw God shining out in a great display of His attributes and proceeded to expound God from the flood in both his epistles.

REFERENCES TO NOAH IN 1 PETER

There was nothing unusual in this, as all was of God in the whole episode of the flood. God spoke, called Noah, commanded to build the ark, and gave the pattern thereof, sent the flood, judged the people, saved Noah and his family, and finally made a covenant with him. All was of God, and Peter laid hold upon this. Great benefit and blessing is bound to be the portion of those who pursue Peter's comments and exposition of the flood, and all things connected with it.

His first reference is in 1 Peter 3:18-22, a difficult and long passage that has baffled many students. It has given rise to many conflicting views, some of them quite fantastic.

The context is suffering; indeed this is the main theme of the first epistle. One can suffer in so many ways, and from so many directions.

1. A Christian can suffer for Christ, owning His Name.
2. A Christian can also suffer for righteousness' sake. Both these aspects of suffering are spoken of by the Lord in Matthew 5:10-11.
3. A Christian can also suffer in ceasing from sin, enduring the temptation instead of succumbing (4:1-2).
4. Also, suffering can come according to the will of God. Job is the great example of this.
5. However, a type of suffering that dare not be entertained is suffering for sin, for wrong doing. The economy of God allows various types of suffering, but not suffering because of sin. This ought not to be; but sad to say it was common in Peter's day and in our own also.

We can follow our Lord in suffering for righteousness' sake. He is our example and we follow His steps (2:21). The Lord also suffered for sins, not His own, but for our sins upon the cross. This is one area of suffering in which we cannot follow our Lord. In this He is not our example but our Saviour. We receive the blessing of His travail upon the cross.

It seems that some of the Christians were doing wrong in Peter's time, were suffering for their deeds, and were even glorying in it. Such suffering was not because of testimony; rather it was the righteous government of God upon them personally, and it often came through the powers that be.

The difficult passage begins with verse 18: "Christ also hath once suffered for sins, the just for the unjust, that He might bring us to God". He died to bring us not merely to heaven, but to fellowship with God, to the enjoyment of walking in the light.

From verse 18 the teaching turns to the flood, a very difficult passage. It is not the intention here to go into the difficulties, especially those in verses 19-20, but to suggest the reason for the passage in the first place.

The saints of Peter's day were passing through much suffering, and were perplexed as to why this was so. If the Spirit has come (1:12) and He is almighty in power, why are so few people embracing the truth of salvation? Why are our numbers so small in comparison with the multitudes that are perishing, and why do we suffer so? Is God not for us?

Peter draws comfort from a comparison with the days of Noah. He uses the material most skilfully to remove all doubt, and to let his readers see that this was to be expected. Noah saw a great movement of the Spirit; it could hardly have been greater for that time, yet the end result was that only eight souls were saved. The rest perished in the flood and are presently in the prison of lost souls. This is just another way of saying the lost souls are now in hell. The people had a visitation of grace: they had a man sent from God, Noah; they heard a message calling them to repentance; they witnessed the preparing of the ark before their very eyes. All was to no avail; there was no response of faith, carelessness marked the people as already observed, and the outcome was that only eight souls were saved.

Now compare this with chapter 1:12, "them that have preached the gospel unto you with the Holy Ghost sent down from heaven; which thing angels desire to look into". Note in passing, that angels were involved in the judgment of the flood in an evil way, but here in 1 Peter 1 in a good way. However, the result was the same as in Noah's day: few responded, so history was repeating itself. So here are two different occasions when the operation of the Spirit was graciously displayed, yet did not yield the expected response.

The second attribute unfolded about God in the passage is the long suffering of God: "The long suffering of God waited in the days of Noah while the ark was a preparing" (v. 20). The message preached was not an invitation to come into the ark as is often thought, but a call to repent from their evil way, and to turn to righteousness: a similar preaching to that of John the Baptist. Just as the people rejected the counsel of God through John against themselves (Luke 7:30), so it was also in Noah's time. The people then are charged with disobedience, "which sometime were disobedient" (v.20). Their disobedience lay not in refusing to enter the ark, as such an invitation was never offered, but in refusing the call to repentance. There was none that responded, not even one. They were so occupied with the social and pleasurable times in which they lived, they must have thought all would go on for ever. Hence, they had no interest in the message. If any were affected at all it was the immediate family of Noah. Salvation came to them

NOAH

not because grace was found in them but because of their link with Noah himself.

Nevertheless, they must have felt the weight of their father's preaching, and kept themselves separated from the current corruption and violence of those times.

Perhaps repentance and a measure of faith were seen in their entering into the ark in obedience to the call of God. As far as the population at large was concerned, they were disobedient in spite of the long suffering of God, who waited so long. God is very patient, "Now the God of patience and consolation grant you to be likeminded (i.e. similarly minded) one towards another according to Christ Jesus" (Rom 15:5). Not only is He patient with saints, but with sinners also, and for long seasons.

Some say that this period of long suffering lasted for 120 years, and base this upon Genesis 6:3, "My Spirit shall not always strive with man for that he also is flesh, yet his days shall be 120 years". However Peter informs us that "the long suffering of God waited while the ark was a preparing", which was less than 100 years. It was this act and the progress of building that condemned the world, as previously noticed. Noah was 500 years old when the Lord first spoke to him, and the flood came when he was 600 years old. So all took place in the between time of 100 years, a long period just the same, and a great display of the long suffering of our God.

The third thing about God that Peter unfolds from the days of the flood is, "God is a Saviour God". Did Noah and his family deserve anything? They were sinners like all men, but they had faith, and God responds to that as in every case of salvation. Paul speaks often in the pastoral epistles of "God our Saviour", and Peter in his second epistle mentions the lovely title "Saviour" no less that five times. How interesting it is that in the closing writings of these great apostles they speak often of God and Christ as Saviour. Both Peter and Paul are near the end of the journey of life (2 Tim 4:6; 2 Pet 1:14), and are occupied not so much with the great doctrines and mysteries of their past ministries, as with the grace of God as Saviour. They were not leaning upon their success in soul winning or in affecting the saints with sound and spiritual teaching, but upon God as Saviour. It is always so; as saints get nearer to their heavenly home the merit of Christ alone fills the heart, the assurance of salvation provided by our Saviour God. From the flood story, Peter unfolds this assuring and comforting fact about God.

A fourth attribute of God in the passage is His righteous judgment. If people persist in disobedience and unbelief, the holy nature of God is offended, and that same nature demands the penalty be paid. The spirits of these contemporaries of Noah are all in prison, hades, suffering the judgment of God for their sins, and greater judgment is to come. Now quite a number of Bible students believe that the Lord Jesus in His spirit went to the place of the departed dead between His death and resurrection, and heralded the triumphs of His death. Not all will not agree with this school of thought, nor is it the view of the present writer, but all agree that the prison of verse 20 is hell, and that the spirits imprisoned there are the careless people that lived prior to the flood. These are the very same people that heard the message of righteousness, that experienced the longsuffering of God, that refused all the grace of God, and were finally taken away by the flood. They had lost their day, now their spirits are in hades. At the time of the writing of the epistle they had been there for thousands of years, and they are there still.

Jude in his single chapter epistle speaks of the people

NOAH

who perished in Sodom and Gomorrah as "suffering the vengeance of eternal fire"; the same is true of those who perished in Noah's day. The highest part of man, according to Paul, is his spirit: "I pray God your whole spirit and soul and body be preserved blameless" (1 Thess 5:23); note that Paul mentions the spirit first. The spirit is the real man dwelling in the body. In some Scriptures the soul has the same idea, and is put for the whole person as in our passage, "eight souls were saved by water". In other Scriptures the soul is used of the quality of life that is lived, as in the classic passage: "What shall it profit a man, if he shall gain the whole world, and lose his own soul" (Mark 8:36). There it speaks of the life as lived unto God or the failing to do so, and can apply as much to a believer as to a sinner.

It is with the human spirit that men worship God (Phil 3:3; Rom 1:9). With many, that spirit, capable of worshipping and serving God, is cast out, rejected and imprisoned to await the judgment because of disobedience to the gospel.

This section of 1 Peter is an example of how to approach any Old Testament passage. There is spiritual meat everywhere in the word of God, and Peter is one who diligently searched it out from the inspired record of Noah.

9

THE FLOOD IN 2 PETER

All second epistles speak of the last days, and 2 Peter is no exception. In doing so, he makes reference to the same conditions prevailing in the days of Noah.

The first reference occurs in chapter 2, where he treats the subject in the same manner as in his first epistle: a display of the attributes and ways of God, especially in judgment upon those who persist in error and unbelief.

His topic is the false teachers of his day whose pernicious teaching was stumbling so many unsaved people who were seeking after the knowledge of God. Naturally, their teaching also wrought havoc among God's believing people. It seemed they were doing so with impunity, that God could not or did not requite it in any way. However, it only seemed that way; but really it was the longsuffering of God: "whose judgment now of a long time lingereth not" (v. 3). The RV renders: "The sentence of judgment now from of old slumbereth not". The sentence was passed upon them a long time ago, and God will eventually carry it out.

Now to support this statement, Peter draws illustrations from three severe judgments of the past when the wrath of God eventually overtook the offenders, although a long time seemingly had passed. Longsuffering came to an end and judgment was the lot of man.

His three examples are all culled from the early chapters of Genesis.

NOAH

1. The angels that sinned, likely Genesis chapter 6.
2. The days of Noah, which is our subject.
3. The destruction of Sodom and Gomorrah, Genesis chapter 19.

The principle always remains, that sin and perversion finally meet their consequences; the just judgment of God must prevail. So Noah and the flood is an example of the judgment of God that finally overtook the offenders.

At this point it would be profitable to consider a parallel passage in the epistle of Jude where he likewise presents three examples of past judgment. Howbeit, there are two differences. Firstly, Peter takes his examples from the record of Genesis, and sets them forth in chronological order. Jude on the other hand does not follow this pattern: he leaves out the case of Noah, and includes the story from Numbers ch. 13: the failure of Israel to enter the land of Canaan. This failure was the result of unbelief, and God manifested His displeasure in that they all died in the wilderness. Secondly, he departs from the chronological order, putting first what happened last, that is, the unbelief of Israel. Look at his three examples.

1. Israel in unbelief: failed to enter the land (Num 13).
2. The angels: kept not their first estate (Gen 6).
3. Sodom and Gomorrah: overthrown (Gen 19).

It is easy to see that the historical order has not been adhered to, rather he adopts a *moral* order. Perhaps that is a deeper view than Peter's.

Jude was a servant working largely in obscurity and overshadowed by his famous brother James. Nevertheless, he was a most intelligent and spiritual man. His wisdom is seen in his ability to present Scripture in a moral order; his teaching is that departure from God has three stages.

Unbelief is the first step of departure as in Hebrews 3:12, "Take heed, brethren, lest there be in any of you an evil heart of unbelief, in departing from the living God". Jude, knowing this, puts the example of unbelief first: a weighty warning to all, although both Jude, and the writer to the Hebrews have in mind unsaved people who refuse the truth.

If unbelief is persisted in, it leads to apostasy, which means the giving up of God. So Jude's next example is the apostasy of the angels that kept not their first estate. Apostasy is the great subject in the epistle of Jude; he feels it must be dealt with. For his last example, he cites Sodom and Gomorrah because they were reprobate, and to be a reprobate according to Romans 1:28, is to be given up by God. The tell tale signs of being reprobate are the unclean practices as seen in Sodom. So the apostate gives up God, whereas one who is reprobate is a stage further on: God has given him up.

Note then his moral order:

1. Unbelief, in departing from God: the example of the failure of Israel.
2. Apostasy, giving God up: seen in the angels that left their first estate.
3. Reprobate, given up by God: the sad example of Sodom and Gomorrah.

Peter, in his second epistle, makes reference to Noah personally, "Noah ... a preacher of righteousness" (2:5). Yet this statement is secondary; his main objective is to present God as capable of judgment; and sooner or later that judgment must fall.

An outstanding contrast springs out of this verse: the

righteous, and the ungodly. Noah practised righteousness in the midst of an ungodly age as Genesis 6 makes clear, but he also preached righteousness as Peter informs us here. He also became heir of the righteousness which is by faith as already considered. So righteousness is a key word with reference to Noah, and he became a suitable witness for God to that past ungodly world. God does not leave Himself without witness in the world. It is always so with God. Even in times of departure in Israel the witness of the prophets was always there, and the greater the departure, the greater the prophet. Elijah and Elisha were such in the terrible days of Jezebel and Ahab. The same could be said of the close of Israel's history in the land. They had turned to gross idolatry, and refused to repent. God raised up a Jeremiah and an Ezekiel in those dark days prior to the captivity.

The mind looks forward to the closing days before the day of the Lord, when the man of lawlessness shall be to the fore, with all his attendant ungodliness. The Lord shall raise up the two witnesses (see Rev 11), as well as the 144000 sealed by God (Rev 7). These shall minister with great power even like that of Elijah.

In the days before the flood Enoch prophesied and Noah preached. These must be the earliest preachers in the Bible, and their witness was against the violent and corrupt ways of their day (Jude 7).

Paul refers to a twofold revelation of God in Romans 11:22, "Behold therefore the goodness and severity of God: on them which fell, severity; but toward thee, goodness". So in this passage Noah experienced the goodness of God: God "saved Noah the eighth person". God was good; all was of grace. Noah recognised this fact in the altar he built to the Lord. He manifested a thankful heart to the Lord, and worshipped.

But the severity of God was also seen, "God spared

THE FLOOD IN 2 PETER

not the old world". There was no mercy offered then; the period of longsuffering was past. When God begins to judge, then His holy nature can make no differences or allowances (see Rom 9:28). This was seen in the judgment of our sin at Calvary: God "spared not his own Son, but delivered him up for us all" (Rom 8:32). The sparing not of the old world was a revelation of righteousness, not of a hard austere God. He cares for people, and takes no pleasure in the death of the wicked. He desires all to be saved. His grace is consistent with His righteousness. God is light, and God is love; both harmonise perfectly. The flood is a demonstration of the goodness and severity of God.

God's power and control are also noticed by Peter in the verse: "*bringing in* the flood upon the world of the ungodly". He enlarges upon this power in the next chapter. Suffice it to state now that the flood was no natural phenomenon, but was caused by the intervention of God. It was announced beforehand to Noah, and he was made to prepare for it. God revealed the very nature of the judgment and that a boat was needed. Also, the timing was set by the Lord, "Yet seven days and I will cause it to rain upon the earth" (Gen 7:4). The Lord was able to change water into wine (John 2:9), and could walk upon the water (John 6:19). He could use water in an everyday way to wash the disciples feet (John 13:5). In the Old Testament, God could change water into blood (Exod 4) and divide the waters of the Red Sea, and those of Jordan (Josh 3-4). He also caused it to rain in the time of harvest in the days of Samuel (1 Sam 12:17), and to show his displeasure, held back the rain for three and a half years in the days of Elijah. In the book of Revelation, reference is made to the angels of the waters (Rev 11:6; 16:5). It is easy in the face of all this to accept that the flood was caused by the power of God Himself; no other

NOAH

explanation is needed.

Another way that God is presented in this passage is that He separates the godly from the ungodly; this is most solemn. In the first psalm, "the ungodly shall not stand... in the congregation of the righteous". The careful reader will observe that the psalm begins and ends with separation. The godly man should separate himself from the counsel of the ungodly while he lives; this is still binding upon all Christians today. The psalm ends with the life to come, when God eternally separates the ungodly from the righteous.

So many Scriptures enforce this solemn lesson, for example Matt 25:46, "these shall go away into everlasting punishment: but the righteous into life eternal". So Peter comes to this conclusion in verse 9: "The Lord knoweth how to deliver the godly out of temptation, and to reserve the unjust unto the day of judgment to be punished". The waters, of the flood separated Noah from that former civilization and his careless, godless contemporaries that perished.

The rapture (1 Thess 4:13-18) will be an intervention of God in the greatest miracle since Calvary, separating the dead in Christ from all the other dead ones. This will be followed by the catching up of all the living Christians with them to meet the Lord in the air. This truly will be a great separation of the living saints from the people they know. All this is prefigured in Enoch, then Noah.

The Lord in His ministry spoke much of the coming separation of saints from sinners: cf. the parable of the two servants, that of the ten virgins, and the parable of the talents. To these could be added from Matthew 13 the parable of the wheat and tares, and that of the good and bad fish. John the Baptist taught the same in the metaphor of the threshing floor, the chaff separated from the wheat. All this is most solemn; it is the teaching

THE FLOOD IN 2 PETER

of Scripture now, but one day it will be a terrible reality for the world.

Peter's next reference is in chapter 3, the most detailed of all his references. Again he brings forth in a beautiful way a wonderful display of God and His attributes.

Peter speaks of the scoffers of his day, and he must have encountered many in his preaching experience. They scoffed especially at the teaching of the Lord's return, and the last days shall see an increase of this scoffing attitude. As Peter points out, they cannot scoff at the past. Human history is full of examples concerning man's sin, mistakes, and the meting out of the judgments which they deserved. It is only fools that close their eyes to the past, and seek to deny the historic Christ, or any other personality of Holy Scripture. However, people can be willingly ignorant as Peter informs here; they just do not want to know. Some people are ignorant having never learned (1 Thess 4:13), but to be willingly ignorant is a worse condition.

"Where is the promise of his coming?" they sneer, then they look back over the past and say, "since the fathers fell asleep, all things continue as they were from the beginning of the creation". Not so, says Peter, what about the flood! Then he makes some enlightening comments about how the wonders of God were displayed at that time.

He first draws attention to the word of God; He speaks and it is done. Creation is in view in verse 5, and specifically the third day (Gen 1:9-12). The scoffers speak of creation, but Peter speaks of its source: God Himself, and the Word: the means of creation. The two verses put side by side picture the earth rising out of the waters: "by the word of God, the heavens were of old, and the earth standing out of the water and in the water" (3:5). "God said, let the waters under the heaven be

NOAH

gathered together unto one place, and let the dry land appear: and it was so. And God called the dry land Earth: and the gathering together of the waters called he Seas" (Gen 1:9-10). In the flood the process was reversed (2 Pet 3:6), again by the Word of God: "Wherein (or as the RV, By which, i.e. by the same Word) the world that then was, being overflowed with water perished". So the word of God is most powerful: He speaks and it is done.

Summing up the New Testament references to Noah: the Lord presents the *times* of Noah, the careless people of that terrible day; Hebrews 11 presents Noah *himself*, the virtue of his faith; Peter unfolds the wonderful way God revealed Himself, a *display of His attributes.*

10

SPIRITUAL TRUTH IN NOAH

There is a great depth of spiritual truth in the narrative of Noah, and again we must go to the epistles of Peter to see this. When expounding the great doctrines of God and of Christianity he often uses this material to illustrate "the things most surely believed among us". Consequently, in 1 Peter 3 and 2 Peter 3 he draws parallels between Noah's day and the coming judgment at the Lord's return. It is plain from 2 Peter 3 that the operative theme is the word of God. God spoke and the terrible judgment of the flood swiftly descended, manifesting God's power over nature. Peter uses this to combat the scoffers who mock at the Bible and the foretelling of future events and to give proof of another, and final, judgment upon this earth. The salient points are these:

1. What God has done before he can do again, i.e. judge the whole world of mankind.
2. It is just as easy for God who has all power over all nature to use fire instead of water, and He will.
3. God has created all things, and it is easier to destroy than to create or build. This can surely be seen today in our world of terrorism. Many beautiful buildings that took great skill and time to erect, disappear in a few seconds by a terrorist bomb. Yes, God created all, which the scoffers will at least acknowledge, and He can so easily destroy all; and He will.

NOAH

4. The all powerful word of God is the same now as it was then, "But the heavens and the earth, which are now, by the same word are kept in store, reserved unto fire against the day of judgment and perdition of ungodly men" (v. 7).

Then he proceeds to describe the day of the Lord as sudden, destructive and final, issuing in the eternal day of God. Therefore a parallel is drawn between the judgment of the flood, and the day of the Lord. It will be remembered that in Matthew 24 the Lord drew such between the days that preceded the flood and those preceding the coming of the Son of man, which of course is the climax of the day of the Lord. Now Peter was present at the Olivet discourse (Mark 13:3) and heard the Lord's comparison of the two times of judgment, and so he develops the subject in this passage.

In point of time the flood is long since past, but it is still an indication and picture of the judgment by fire soon to come. Consider a few parallels in the two judgments.

The corruption and violence of the people had reached such a level as to demand the judgment of the flood; God in righteousness had to intervene. Now it is a principle in God's dealings with mankind to give evil time to develop, and if repentance is lacking, to judge the evil when it is come to the full. It was so in Genesis 15:16, "The iniquity of the Amorites is not yet full". But it was full over 400 years later, and then the Lord used Israel to punish them, and gave them their land. Again, in the parable of the tares and wheat, the command was given not to uproot the tares but to let both grow together until the harvest (Matt 13:29-30). Also with the prodigal son, the father did not stop him in his evil design; sin increasingly developed in the many downward steps.

However, repentance came about and all ended well; the judgment was averted. In the final recompense for sin, as the final conflict approaches, John is informed that, "the harvest of the earth is ripe" (Rev 14:15). Then the flaming sword of judgment shall be revealed. To the angel is given the command, "Thrust in thy sickle, and reap: for the time is come for thee to reap; for the harvest of the earth is ripe". When we see the sin of corruption, violence and falsehood advancing at an alarming rate, surely the harvest is almost ripe for the sickle of God's judgment. As in the past, so in the future there will be an increasing condition of sin that finally will reach a stage when judgment can be no longer stayed.

Another similarity in the two judgments is that the godly are warned beforehand. Noah was warned of God of things not seen as yet, and how much does the New Testament warn of the day of the Lord, and of the signs that will be a voice to the godly that live in those last days. The words of Paul to the Thessalonians are fitting here, "But of the times and the seasons, brethren, ye have no need that I write unto you. For yourselves know perfectly that the day of the Lord so cometh as a thief in the night... But ye, brethren, are not in darkness, that that day should overtake you as a thief" (1 Thess 5:1-4). They knew of the coming day of the Lord, and they were first century Christians. How much more do the Christians presently on the earth see the signs on every hand, and are therefore warned. Much more will it be so in the tribulation days just prior to the great event of the day of the Lord. The saints are called "sons of the light and sons of the day" (1 Thess 5:5); they belong to that company that have been enlightened by God, and will have their inheritance in the day of God of which Peter speaks.

Again, Noah preached to the people soon to be destroyed; they heard a message. Today the prophetic

NOAH

word is being sounded out in thousands of pulpits all over the world. Alas, sometimes preachers of the gospel omit from their messages the great subject of the Lord's return. The prophetic word concerns all nations, and is final.

Further, the past judgment was by water; according to Peter, the future one will be with fire. The Lord simply uses the earth's own resources to bring about its destruction. This is now known by all to be only too possible, considering the potential of the atomic and hydrogen bombs of today. Man now has the power to destroy all, and this is no doubt permitted in the counsels of God who sits upon the throne of glory. God will use the fearful unleashing of this energy in the final dissolution of all things by fire. In 2 Peter 3:10, the fisherman of old speaks like a modern scientist when he uses such language as, "The elements shall melt with fervent heat". The Lord is in control of all. The Book of Revelation speaks of the angels of the waters, which no doubt were active in Noah's day, and the angels of fire will be active in the coming judgment by fire. It would be profitable at this stage to point out that the day of the Lord is an extended period covering a little over 1000 years. It commences with the manifestation of the Son of man in the heavens (Matt 24:29-30) and ends at the close of the millennium. The final Satanic revolt (Rev 20:7-10), and the convulsion of fire spoken of by Peter, end the millennium. Paul speaks of the commencement of the day of the Lord, coming as a thief (1 Thess 5:2), whereas Peter tells us of the end of the day of the Lord in the passing away of the heavens and the earth issuing forth to the day of God which is eternal.

Again similar statements are made of both judgments concerning the word of God, that awesome authority that controls all, and which can reserve and unleash

SPIRITUAL TRUTH IN NOAH

judgment in His own way and time. The One that created all things, now upholds "all things by the word of His power" (Heb 1:3) and in speaking, will close all in judgment. Hebrews 12:25-7 could well be cited here. "See that ye refuse not him that speaketh. For if they escaped not who refused him that spake on earth, much more shall not we escape, if we turn away from him that speaketh from heaven; whose voice then shook the earth: but now he hath promised, saying, Yet once more I shake not the earth only, but also heaven. And this word, Yet once more, signifeth the removing of those things that are shaken, as of things that are made, which those things that cannot be shaken may remain".

The things that remain are the things of the kingdom of God, and the new creation. The controlling power of the Word is seen also in Israel's experience in the wilderness, when in unbelief they refused to enter into the land. The Lord swore in His wrath that they should not enter into the land, and all that generation fell as corpses in the wilderness, with the exception of Joshua and Caleb. God speaks and it is done; nothing can disobey His command. So it was with the past flood, and so it will be in the future passing away of the present world.

A "no escape" policy is common to both judgments: "the flood came, and took them all away" (Matt 24:39). All flesh and everything that moved perished in the Genesis account. The number that perished we do not know, but some suggest that the population of the earth was rekoned in millions at that time. This we do know that only eight people were saved. Paul in teaching about the day of the Lord, writes similarly concerning the ungodly: For when they shall say, Peace and safety; then sudden destruction cometh upon them, as travail upon a woman with child; and they shall not escape" (1

NOAH

Thess 5:3). Many shall die in the final days of trouble, wars and pestilence; the tribulation shall be the means of removing many apostates both Jews and Gentiles. The great battle of Armageddon shall destroy millions of the ungodly with their military might. Then the Lord shall set up the throne of His glory and shall judge the nations that remain; none shall escape. The goats, speaking of the unbelievers, shall be separated from the believers, seen under the figure of sheep. The righteous judgment of God catches up with everyone without the salvation which is in Christ.

As "the longsuffering of God waited in the days of Noah, while the ark was a preparing" (1 Pet 3:20), so the longsuffering of God is now waiting while the Lord builds His church (Matt 16). Peter, who speaks of ark building also speaks of the spiritual building of the temple which is the church: "Ye also, as living stones, are built up a spiritual house" (1 Pet 2:5). The process has been going on for a long time and the lengthy period is attributed to God's longsuffering in 2 Peter 3:9. "The Lord is not slack concerning his promise, as some men count slackness: but is longsuffering to us-ward, not willing that any should perish". But the flood marked the end of God's patience and the beginning of His wrath; so will it be in the coming of the Son of man. Gospel preachers today ought to keep this in mind and preach with earnestness and sincerity, knowing that time is short. The period of longsuffering will soon terminate; grace cannot go on for ever.

How gracious it is of our God that in both judgments He remembers mercy. Out of the flood came eight saved souls: salvation is a blessed experience. Similarly out of the great tribulation shall come a great multitude which no man can number, each one will have washed his robes in the blood of the Lamb and will enter into the joy

(Rev 7:14). The same can be said of the judgment of the nations in Matthew 25; the sheep going into the kingdom represent those saved during the terrible times. Of course it will also be true of Israel's awakening as the nation is born in a day: "There shall come out of Sion the Deliverer, and shall turn away ungodliness from Jacob" (Rom 11:26). Salvation is common to both judgments.

One final thought concerning the similar pattern of the two judgments is that a better world emerges in both cases. We will leave the comments to be made upon Noah's new world until the Genesis record is being considered. Suffice it to say that it was very different from the days before the flood. The promise of God, the covenant, the worship, the government and the greater variety of food brought a new age to Noah and his family. To borrow Peter's words. "The world that then was perished". He also informs us that this present world shall pass away: "Nevertheless we, according to his promise, look for new heavens and a new earth, wherein dwelleth righteousness" (2 Pet 3:13). John would say, Amen, to this: "And I saw a new heaven and a new earth: for the first heaven and the first earth were passed away; and there was no more sea" (Rev 21:1). So a new state of things replaces the old after both judgments.

However a few distinguishing contrasts can be observed. On the one hand the new world came out of water, and on the other, out of fire. Again, in Noah's new world sin and death still reigned, and new laws were created to curb evil. So while it was a better world it was far from perfect. Sin increased until it reached that sad level commented upon in Romans 1. Wrath was revealed from heaven and was about to fall upon a sinful world. Instead of judging that world, God moved in grace and provided salvation in Christ, inaugurating this present period of grace, and the world experienced a reprieve.

NOAH

Contrast the new heaven and earth where righteousness dwells. All evil is forever gone and righteousness makes its eternal home there. How beautiful that righteousness merely reigns in the millennium. Evil will still exist and must be kept down. But in the day of God all will be perfect. No sin, no death, nor the fear of another fall can be there to mar God's fair creation. Alas in that new world of Noah's there was sin such as the drunkenness of Noah himself, blemish in at least one of his sons, and another curse added. Perfection will not come until the new creation dawns and God dwells there.

Notice how the apostle Peter follows his lesson from the days of Noah with some exhortations linked with things spoken of Noah. Noah was moved by fear concerning "things not seen as yet". The same idea is implied in 2 Peter 3:15, "We, according to his promise *look for* new heavens and a new earth,". The big difference of course is that we are moved by love and not by fear as in the case of Noah. There it was wrath, here it is grace. All our hope is based upon the love we know God has for His own. Noah in a sense feared the future, we look forward to the longed for blessing of God.

Also in view of these promises we are to be without spot and blameless (v. 14). Again these very things describe Noah in Genesis 6. He was a just man, that is before men, which is the same as being blameless. It is possible to be blameless before men. The Lord can see the slightest spot. Blamelessness is manward; spotlessness is generally Godward. With this Genesis 6 agrees again. God said that Noah was "perfect" in his generations. The word translated 'perfect' is the same word used to describe Israel's lamb in Exod 12 and translated "Without blemish". This brought the favour of God upon Noah. It is so today with God's believing people. To be just is before men; to be without blemish before God is to be in the circle of His favour in light of His soon return.

Again, Peter adds a solemn warning in v. 17: "Beloved, seeing ye know these things before, beware lest ye also, being led away with the error of the wicked, fall from your own stedfastness". Now Noah knew the Lord's displeasure upon those that indulged in the lust of the flesh, yet he was careless about the same in himself. "Beware", is just what Noah failed to do; he indeed fell from his own steadfastness; he was drunken and was found naked by his sons. Alas for failure in old age! It is one thing to start well, but another to end well. It was sad to see Noah in such a predicament in his closing years, and bringing a curse upon some of his grandchildren. Peter would have us progress all the time: "But grow in grace, and in the knowledge of our Lord and Saviour Jesus Christ" (V. 18).

It is now time to leave this chapter in which Peter uses material from Noah to bring home to the heart the closing events of our earth, and the eternal new heavens and earth that surely will be realities some day.

11

BAPTISM IN 1 PETER 3

1 Peter 3 must be considered in a similar way to 2 Peter 3 where the writer draws spiritual truth and Christian ethics from the writings concerning Noah. Again, the same principle is followed: he uses the Genesis record not only to declare the ways and glory of God, but also as shadows of the greater things to come in the New Testament revelation. The context and thought flow of the chapter must be considered to see the truth, and the great incentive to holy living against the background of Noah.

It is well-known that suffering is a leading theme in 1 Peter. It is quite in order for a saint to experience certain sufferings, such as suffering for righteousness' sake or for Christ. However, to suffer because of sin or wrong doing is another thing. We are not to bring trouble upon ourselves because of foolish or wrong behaviour. This is an avenue in which we could not follow our Lord for He never trod it; He suffered for sin not His own, for He never sinned, nor could He. Peter puts the matter well in 2:22-24, "Who did no sin, neither was guile found in his mouth;...Who his own self bare our sins in his own body on the tree". Again, in verse 18 of our chapter, "Christ also hath once suffered for sins,... being put to death in the flesh". But one might say, "Look, I have an old nature still as well as that divine nature of which I am a partaker (2 Pet 1:4), and sometimes that old nature overcomes me and manifests itself in wrong doing". After all, Peter himself denied with oaths and cursing that he knew the Lord; he failed to witness and told lies to protect himself. God has made strong provision for us that we should not sin, and this he unfolds for us here. Look at Noah and see an interesting and encouraging thing: his experience is a type of a God given provision so that a believer can largely refrain from sin and cease to grieve his Lord. Noah was separated by water from the old world with all its sin, blasphemy, corruption and violence. After the flood he could not go back to that world; it had died to him. It could be said that water saved him from the old life, from the company of the unsaved that formerly compassed him about. In like figure, or through the same element, *water,* the believer is now saved from sinning. Baptism in water is the antitype (RV margin) of the flood. Let us examine this teaching.

First he tells us what baptism is not: there is no power in it to save the soul, no virtue to put away sin. The answer to sin is given in chapter one: the blood of Christ. This alone prevails before God, so baptism is not a putting away of the sins of the flesh. Then he tells us what baptism really is, and how it can be of great benefit to the believer in his struggle against sin. He has drawn from the flood the point that water saved Noah and deduced by analogy that water can save the believer from the power of sin and lead to a sanctified life. His argument is as follows. The Lord Jesus has been raised from the dead, and has gone back to heaven, back to God (v. 22). The saint also has been brought to God (v. 18). So we are as Christ; Peter here touches on Ephesian truth. Our position now is that we are raisen with Christ and placed in Him having first died in Him. Now if the believer is tempted to sin this position, as expressed in baptism, can be a great help to him, a reminder indeed of that placing in Christ by God Himself. It is expressed here as, "the answer of a good conscience towards God". The good conscience is that we are dead in Christ and raised with Him to that position He now occupies. All this came about by our embracing the gospel. In the past, Israel with their offerings had always the conscience of sins (Heb 10:1-3). They were different from the man in Christ, and the heart possessed by Christ. He has a good conscience before God. The word translated "answer" in the AV is a legal word, and would be better rendered "interrogation" as in the RV This is how it would work out in practice.

The temptation arises in the heart of a believer to sin. Then he could ask himself questions, or better still, God could interrogate him as follows.

Are you dead in Christ? Yes, I am.
Are you baptized in symbol of this death? Yes, I am.
Would a dead man commit this sin; could one who is dead possibly do this thing? No, he could not.

The same argument and answer is found in Romans 6:7, "he that is dead is freed from sin or, hath ceased from sin".

Again, can a man in Christ, one in the heavenlies, do this thing, and so sin against the Lord in heaven? No, he can not, as there is no sin in heaven: "there shall in no wise enter into it any thing that defileth" (Rev 21:27). The result is that the saint feels that he can not do this thing, and sin against God. In fact it is morally impossible to sin in the temptation if the good conscience before God is there. So he has been saved from sinning; his baptism has saved him. As the water of the flood saved Noah from the old life, so does the water of our baptism save us from the life we once lived as men alive to sin.

Therefore, Peter can see in the experience of Noah a type of the baptised believer today, and his position in Christ expressed by the water of baptism. The water is not magic, rather it is the symbol of the great experience of being placed by God in the glorified Christ, and the application of this truth.

In 2 Peter 2 also the apostle makes a comparison between the times of Noah and those in which Peter lived. The chapter is an exposure of false teachers. Judgment on them seems to tarry, but three examples are cited to assure us that the judgment of God will eventually catch up with the false teachers. In verse 5 he describes Noah as a preacher of righteousness; his preaching was similar to that of the gospel preacher today: the righteousness of God that is found in Christ, and the practical outcome in the life of the one who believes.

Noah preached that the people of his day should abstain from the unrighteous corruption that was the norm of the times, but the greater gospel bestows an imputed righteousness on him that believes that can stand before the throne of God. This new life is bound to be manifested to the world around in the moral behaviour of the believers.

Now all NT doctrine can be classified under three headings: the cross, the church and the coming of the Lord. For instance, the Gospels, Romans and Galatians are mostly to do with the salvation of the soul, and so come under the cross. Ephesians, Colossians, and Philippians are the great revelation of the church which is His body, so the common theme is the church. The Thessalonian epistles and the Revelation have the coming of the Lord as the chief theme, so come under the coming. Now note Peter's three references to Noah. 2 Peter 2 relates to the gospel and the error that would oppose it. Clearly its catagory is the cross. In 1 Peter 3

NOAH

the subject of christian baptism is to do with our position in Christ, and so with the church. This was of course the great commission in Matthew 28, to teach all nations. Finally, in 2 Peter 3 Noah is linked with the soon coming of our Lord Jesus and the judgment that will surely follow. It belongs to the coming.

We have come to the conclusion of the NT references to Noah, his day, and the great flood. It now remains to approach the actual record in Genesis 5:28 to 9:29. It would be sound practice to follow the line of the NT writers. That is to examine first the character of the times and people as did the Lord; then to consider the man Noah himself as the writer of the Hebrew epistle did; and finally to look for the display of the Lord in the whole episode. This we will do if the Lord permit.

12

THE EVIL PEOPLE IN GENESIS 4

The progress of the natural man and the spiritual man can be traced in the genealogies of Genesis 4 and 5. Chapter 4 contains that of Cain, chapter 5 that of Seth; both were sons of Adam. Now it is evident that the line of Cain desired life to be as attractive and comfortable as possible without God. They went about that very task, building the first city, a progressive and seemingly happy place, but without any teaching or communion with their Creator. The opposite appears in the line of Seth; the godly character emerges and is very much to the fore. They recognise that the Lord exists, and they have great responsibility in that direction. The Spirit inspired Moses, the writer of Genesis, to record their genealogies in an entirely different way from that of Cain. The order also is significant in that Cain's line comes first, following the principle of 1 Corinthians 15:46, "Howbeit that was not first which is spiritual, but that which is natural; and afterward that which is spiritual".

Cain went out from the presence of the Lord (v.16), a deliberate turning away from God; a very dangerous action it proved to be. It lead to the developing of all the evil imaginations of the heart, removing all restraint from the ethics that would have been binding if he had rather turned to the Lord. It opened the door to degenerating behaviour that culminated in the flood. He dwelt in the land of Nod which means "Wandering", a name so descriptive of his godless behaviour. The same

NOAH

is true of all that reject the gospel, and as wandering sheep stray away from the Lord. The parables in Luke 15, the wandering sheep and the son going into the far country away from the father's house, are typical of the attitude of Cain. Chapter 3 ends with God driving out the man, Adam, but the hostility of the unregenerate heart is seen in Cain: he went out from the presence of the Lord. The opposite is true of the believer. "The world is crucified unto me, and I unto the world" is the great confession of the apostle Paul in Galatians 6:14. I do not want the world, nor does the world want me; we are dead to each other, is what he means. The attitude of this world, despising all that is of God and pursuing its own interests, is the attitude of Cain, and such is the nature of man, his legacy from the terrible fall. In contrast, the Christian ought to shun the world, finding better things, and greater joy in Christ. Therefore, this Cain is the progenitor of a posterity, continuing to the present day, that does not reckon with God in any of its affairs.

Family life appears in verse 17, a son is born. Cain then builds a city and calls it Enoch, after the name of his son. How typical it is that Cain should seek to promote his son. Such is the way of mankind. Alas, the family is exalted to such a degree that the things of God become very dim and unimportant. Sad to say this is often traced in the families of believers. How unfitting in christian company to hear a constant stream of words in praise of one's offspring rather than speaking of the grace of God and the treasures of His word. All our sons and daughters were born in sin, and this we ought to remember. If grace has saved some of them, we ought to be taken up with that grace. The mother of James and John fell into this snare, requesting a prominent position for her boys in the coming kingdom (Matt 20:20-23). She obviously thought her boys were more worthy than the rest of the

THE EVIL PEOPLE IN GENESIS 4

disciples, and this place was rightfully theirs. It would seem she had planted the same thoughts in the minds of the sons; they request the same thing. The Lord addressed the two sons, asking them, "Can you drink of my cup, and be baptized with my baptism?" They answer, "Yes". It is evident that they had as much self confidence as Peter had. Later when the test came, "they all forsook him and fled" (Matt 26:56).

This same snare comes out in a very interesting story in Judges 17. A woman had the misfortune of being robbed of 1100 shekels of silver, quite a sum of money. She pronounced a curse upon the head of the thief who had done such a terrible thing. The thief turned out to be her own son, and the money was for the production of an idol. She blessed him, "Blessed be thou of the Lord my son". This failure to see evil in one's own children is first seen in Cain, and his son Enoch.

Cain built a city, something solid that for a while will resist the ravages of time. How different was Abraham the pilgrim; he left the city to dwell in a tent, a temporary thing. How beautiful is the comment of Hebrews 11 on this, "dwelling in tabernacles with Isaac and Jacob, the heirs with him of the same promise: For he looked for a city which hath foundations, whose builder and maker is God" (vv. 9,10). Cities in the Bible are generally evil, as Sodom and Gomorrah, and the cities concerning which the Lord spoke such words of judgment: "Woe unto thee, Chorazin! woe unto thee, Bethsaida!" (Matt 11:21). These had seen the mighty works of the Lord Jesus and had not repented. The last great city of this earth will be Babylon (Rev 18) and can be compared with the first city, of Cain's building. Both are cities of this world, with nothing in them for God, yet both have tremendous influence on the populations of their day.

Cain called the city "Enoch" after his son to keep the

NOAH

name of his son alive. Men try to obscure the knowledge that death removes all; they try in some way to remain, at least in name. Such is the world of today. Many cities, buildings and airports are named after men who were great in the eyes of the world. With Cain it seems to have been a kind of defiance of death, "You can take us, but you cannot remove our name nor our memorial from the earth". Surely it is better to have your name written in heaven than upon the earth. With such a thought the Lord inspired the disciples in Luke 10: "rejoice not that the spirits are subject unto you; but rather rejoice, because your names are written in heaven" (v. 20). This was to make the disciples glory in the power of grace rather than in their own power over the demons. It is wonderful to consider that while so many of the saints are unknown and obscure on earth, they are not strangers to heaven; their names are written there.

Verse 19 introduces another feature in this catalogue of wordly ways: Lamech took two wives. Here is the beginning of the corruption that soon filled the whole earth, and brought about the conditions that demanded the flood. The lust of the flesh was at work, so one wife was not enough. This surely was the forerunner of the unfaithfulness and divorce that have so marked the morals of the people increasingly to this day.

Another thing that emerges is the prominent place given to the woman. Three are mentioned in this list which is very much the exception in Bible genealogies. Matthew 1 is very different. The names of four women appear there in the genealogy of our Lord. This is a wonderful exhibition of grace, as each had a blemish upon her character. Paul makes mention of "those women... whose names are in the book of life" (Phil 4:3). It is worthy of note that no female names occur in chapter 5, but here, besides the two wives of Lamech,

THE EVIL PEOPLE IN GENESIS 4

Adah and Zillah, a third woman appears, Naamah. Naamah means beauty; the emphasis is on *looks* and perhaps there was the first attempt at cosmetics. So wives and women are prominent as taking an active part in all that is being done. That women have a great place of service in the economy of God is well demonstrated by many examples in Scripture, women of spiritual renown such as Ruth, Deborah and Esther, to say nothing of the great women in the Gospels that ministered unto the Lord of their substance. The information in chapter 4 is different: it is the setting aside of the headship in the man.

The genealogy of Seth that commences in v. 25 stands in contrast, in that no female name is mentioned at all. They believed in headship which is insisted upon in 1 Corinthians 11:2-3 and 1 Timothy 2:11-15. Nevertheless, Christianity has given more liberty to the woman than all the customs and religions of the heathen past and present.

Verses 20 to 22 describe the development of society. This is seen in three ways, firstly in possessions and trade (v. 20). The tents of Jabal are not in contrast to the city of Cain's making, nor do they set forth pilgrim character as in Abraham, rather do they depict commerce, the accommodation of people that travel in pursuit of trade. They would buy cattle in one place, move on to another area and there sell the cattle at a profit. Even to this day in the Middle East the Bedouins live in tents, moving from place to place, but are by no means poor. The people of this genealogy have no substance in heaven so they go in for possessions upon the earth. The rich fool of Luke 12 and the rich man of Luke 16 are both warnings given by the Lord against covetousness, which can be the cause of one forfeiting the true riches. The words there are weighty: "Take heed, and beware of

93

covetousness: for a man's life consisteth not in the abundance of the things which he possesseth" (Luke 12:15).

There follows the development of entertainment in Jubal, the father of all such as handle the harp and organ, and string and wind instruments. Now music is loved by so many, including believers, and is much set by in the Psalms and in the worship of the temple. Again, in the heavenly scenes in the Revelation, mention is made of harps, trumpets and voices singing. But here they produce pleasure for the natural man without God. Skill today in the music world is not only a means of becoming famous, a well known celebrity, but chiefly a way to quick riches. A weird sort of music is one of Satan's tools for holding of the minds of the masses of the young people. Note in the passage that it was not Tubal himself but his sons and daughters, the younger generation, that became the music makers. Among the richest people today are the Pop Stars, and the music they produce is the means of holding millions of people, especially the young generation, at a distance from God. To follow the music stars of the day goes hand in hand with the rejection of Christ as Lord and Saviour. All the world follows one of two men, either Christ, or the Antichrist. It is sad when believers get caught up in this, and have an ear for the sounds of the music of this world and so little interest in hearing the word of God, and the Spirit's voice searching the conscience.

The third item depicting the progress of man is the use of invention and art to make an easier and more pleasant world for the natural man. According to verse 22 Zillah bore Tubal-cain, and he become the forger of every cutting instrument of brass and iron, tools to produce all manner of works. It is wonderful what advancements there have been from then till now, and still inventions of all sorts are toppling out from the fertile minds of men.

Now these inventions we can use without abusing them. On the other hand we do not need to be so taken up with them that the spiritual life is sapped dry. This is the plan of the enemy of the souls of men. Good music is sweet, and can have a calming effect upon the mind as in the case of king Saul. Inventions are very acceptable and have improved life in a variety of ways. The problem in Genesis 4 was not the things in themselves that made life easier, but their attitude of total independence of God.

"All things are lawful for me, but all things edify not", says the apostle in 1 Corinthians 10:23. Today the world without God is interested in things not people, and certainly not God. How sad it is to pass one's life occupied with things, and then to pass on to eternity with nothing.

Such was the progress right up to the time of the flood, they went their own way as wandering sheep running headlong into the wrath and judgment of God.

Another trend is introduced in Lamech, that takes away the good of progress, that is violence (vv. 23-4). He was a law unto himself, so producing lawlessness and becoming a forerunner of the man of lawlessness in 2 Thessalonians 2. A young man hurt him, so Lamech killed him. He laid aside the law given to Cain in verse 15 of this chapter, which later was formalised to Noah (Gen 9:5-6), and which by instinct ought to have been in the conscience of Lamech. Without any word from God he took a life, and merely because the young man hurt him. The punishment went so far beyond the crime; he took it into his own hand to touch the sacred life of another, and without a just cause.

But Lamech also boasts of this awful deed, his

punishment is more severe than God's to the slayer of Cain: "If Cain shall be avenged sevenfold, truly Lamech seventy and sevenfold". It was as if he had said "You can break God's laws and offend Him if you like with little comeback, but you had better beware of me, I am very much more severe". This was the start of the chain of violence that demanded the judgment of the flood. It has increased in our own day and soon will be closed in the more severe judgment of fire spoken of by Peter.

Note too, that while he clearly refers to God in his boastful statement, he does not actually mention God or refer to His name. Men have developed a language that leaves God out. "God is not in all his thoughts" (Ps 10:4). This later developed into mocking God and taking His name in vain. The only way the ungodly of our day refer to God is by swearing, oaths, and blasphemy; there is no fear of God before their eyes.

Now in Lamech appears also oratory and poetry. The violent act is dressed up in lovely words to make the deed look right and necessary, and so to take away from the guilt of the crime. The same tactic is often used especially in the political scene; clever speeches becloud evil deeds that would horrify most people. Political causes that can sometimes be most evil are veiled in attractive words. His audience was his wives, they would favour him, they would feel proud to be wives of such a famous man: "Hear my voice, ye wives of Lamech, hearken unto my speech". Alongside this is the art of today; so much uncleanness is condoned as being artistic, and so covers the shame of all that is done, especially in the entertainment world. Poetry too can be most attractive, but it can also contain matter that is obscene and ought not to be brought to the minds of people. The printing press turns out an abundance of material that is obscene and dangerous, which warps the minds of

THE EVIL PEOPLE IN GENESIS 4

young people, and projects sin against God and man as sweet morsels to be enjoyed in modern living.

Finally there is the subtle mockery of God as if God cannot avenge but Lamech can. God is too soft, Lamech is a force to be reckoned with. Thus there is the setting aside of the government of God in the earth, although that government goes steadily on while they know it not. The flood was the result of this government. It is interesting that Peter's epistles carry the theme of the government of God intervening in the affairs of men, and make many references to the flood as seen in an earlier chapter. He also speaks of the mockers of the last days as they say, "Where is the promise of his coming?" This is the Lamech attitude, which is prevalent today, and will later develop in that period called the Last Days.

Such is the development from Cain to the flood: the world comfortable without God, and increasing in violence and corruption as seen in Lamech. All this evil had increased to such a degree that when God in grace sent a messenger, Noah the preacher of righteousness, all his efforts went unheeded. Consequently, they were left to the doom of the flood.

13

THE SPIRITUAL MAN OF GENESIS CHAPTER 5

Chapter 5 is the second list of names, being the genealogy of Seth, and reminds us again of that principle, "First the natural, as seen in Cain, after that the spiritual, appearing in Seth". Our purpose is not to go down the passage verse by verse as in chapter 4, but rather to glean some general principles that mark the spiritual man. These run throughout the chapter, and are very important to the believer.

In verse 1 the *creation* is acknowledged. How clear and distinct is this: "In the day that God created man", and how unlike the man of chapter 4 who rebels against the knowledge of God. To the spiritual, God is the source of all, and is fundamental to all his thinking.

The *fall* is freely acknowledged also, as can be noticed by comparing verse 1 with verse 3. Man before the fall was in the likeness of God: "In the likeness of God made he him" (v. 1), but the change in verse 3 is instructive, "Adam... begat a son in his own likeness". Between these verses the fall has taken place, and man has lost the likeness of God. The NT speaks of man as still being in the image of God (1 Cor 11:7), but nowhere in the writings of the NT is the *likeness* of God attributed to fallen man. It would seem that *image* carries the idea of position, as having the ability to rule, and that is still with the man, but *likeness* seems to be moral, and man lost this through the fall. This explains why God drove out man from Eden and from the fellowship of Himself. When the likeness was lost, the man had nothing in common with God. Only a sacrificial death could restore this, and so we shall be like His Son (Phil 3:20-21), not only in glorious condition but in moral standing as well. How thankful we are for the sacrifice offered on Calvary's Cross and accepted by God. So the fall of man is freely accepted here.

Headship is also adhered to. The peculiar language of verse 2 presents this truth, "Male and female created he them... and called their name Adam", which means man (RV). The female was Eve, but her name is omitted. In fact no woman's name appears in this list; all are men, and the women are completely hidden. No doubt they fulfilled their calling in the birth of their children, but their names and themselves are not mentioned at all. The contrast with chapter 4 is clearly seen, where the names of three prominent women appear: Adah, Zillah, and Naamah.

Another point very much emphasised here is *time*. Again there is no mention of this in chapter 4, but in the line of Seth time is measured by days and years. The length of the life of each of the characters of this chapter is told in years, and repeated throughout. Consider a few practical points.

1. They realised they were only upon this earth for a little while; their lives were governed by time. Thoughts of time lead to thoughts of eternity, and the brevity of time becomes a conviction. This changes the outlook on many other things as 2 Corinthians 4:18 says, "we look not at the things which are seen, but at the things which are not seen: for the things which are seen are temporal; but the things which are not seen are eternal".

NOAH

2. It is a good thing also to learn to value time, and make the most of it. "Redeeming the time", says the apostle Paul in Ephesians 5:16, and again, "time is short" in 1 Corinthians 7:29. Peter the apostle, with whole heartedness agrees with this in 1 Peter 4:3, "For the time past of our life may suffice us to have wrought the will of the Gentiles", and verse 2 "That he no longer should live *the rest of his time* in the flesh to the lusts of men, but to the will of God". In the genealogy of chapter 5 each man in his time produced something for God in the seed royal that lead up to the Christ.
3. In the case of Methuselah another time note appears in the meaning of his name, "When he is dead it shall come" meaning the flood. These were aware of the times and the signs of the times, understanding that things were heading up to a climax.

In Luke 12:56 the Lord upbraided the people and religious leaders because though they could discern the weather from the sky, they could not discern "this time", that is the time of their visitation in grace. This, and other passages uttered by the Lord and the apostles, use the word time to express divine movements in grace or in judgment. So the godly of Genesis 5 take note of the prophetic times, and can discern the movements of God. This is especially seen in Enoch who walked with God for three hundred years after the birth of Methuselah (v. 22). There seems to have been a communication of some sort from God at the birth of the boy concerning his name and its meaning. At any rate the whole life of Enoch was altered, a real conversion story.

In our times we name our children after some near relative or friend, or just give them the name we fancy, but the Bible characters named their children in an entirely different way. Sometimes the name was suggested by the circumstances during the birth, as in the case of Ichabod in 1 Samual 4:21, or by the aspiration of the parents, as Eve named Cain, hoping he was a man from the Lord. But some also were named by the unusual method of divine communication as was John the Baptist, and of course the Lord Jesus Himself in Matthew 1:21. At least Enoch responded to the communication from the Lord, and his wonderful walk began; it lasted consistently for 300 years. The people at the birth of a greater than Methuselah, even Christ, refused to come to Him who had the power to save His people from their sins.

By a little simple arithmetic it will become clear that the warning given at the birth of Methuselah was precisely carried out. He lived to be 969 years old. When he begot Lamech he was 187, and Lamech was 182 when Noah was born in the 369th year of the life of Methuselah. Adding to this 600 years, being the age of Noah when the flood came, brings the total to 969 years. So it appears that Methuselah died the same year that the flood came upon the earth. The believer can certainly apply this to himself: does he recognise the times in which his lot is cast? The last days are upon us and the filling up of sin, leading to the events that shall issue in the coming of the Lord. Indeed the Lord, in referring to the times of Noah, exhorted that a *watching spirit* should characterise saints at the time.

For Enoch, God had something better even than being preserved through the flood: he was taken, raptured, God took him. He was a most remarkable man in that he was the first in the Bible to walk with God, and the first to prophesy as Jude 14 informs us, and the first man to be raptured. The earth was very corrupt, and God had no place in it, but Enoch is able to give God his company, and they walk together apart from this world.

NOAH

Another great difference in this genealogy from that of chapter 4, is that *death* is continually mentioned. The little phrase "and he died" is repeated in verses 5, 8, 11, 14, 17, 20, 27 and 31. They take notice that they are only on earth for a little while, although they lived to great ages. To them death was a reality, whereas the people in chapter 4 sought to cloud it over. Neither their age nor the fact of their death is recorded, except the murder of the young man. In a way the folk of chapter 5 were saying, "This world is not my home"; this kept them from living in a fool's paradise.

Another point of interest that could easily be missed is that the word "died" occurs *eight* times in the passage, which is the number of resurrection or a new beginning. With Abraham the covenant was confirmed by the circumcision of his son Isaac on the eighth day. In like manner Zachariah the priest in Luke 1 was of the order of Abijah, the eighth course, when the angel appeared and announced the new beginning in the birth of John. Later he prophesied of that new beginning at the end of the chapter. So while these died, they looked for resurrection, and the new beginning of the inheritance with God. The words of Hebrews 11:13 could well be written over them, "These all died in faith", and they could surely say, "O death, O grave, I do not dread your power". Truly this world was not their home.

Again, apart from their births, their families, ages, and deaths, nothing else is recorded. The absence of possessions, inventions and progress is remarkable. What they did in everyday life is not recorded; it matters little. What they accomplished for God is known by God, and that is what really matters. The exception to this was Enoch; he walked with God. No doubt the others did also, but Enoch is singled out because of the birth of Methuselah and the ensuing rapture.

THE SPIRITUAL MAN OF GENESIS CHAPTER 5

Cain's offspring walked with the world, enjoying its possessions, entertainments and the things that are seen, walking amidst the corruption and violence as being part of it. These others walked apart from the world in fellowship with the Lord.

Now it will be noticed that there is an Enoch in both chapters, one of each lineage, but they are entirely different from each other. The name means "dedicated". The Enoch of chapter 4 was dedicated to keeping his name alive upon the earth in a city named after him. The Enoch of chapter 5 looked for a city which had foundations, whose builder and maker was God (Heb 11:10). The one looked at the things which are seen, and temporal, the other at the things not seen, and eternal. Strange as it may seem, it is the Enoch of chapter 5 that is remembered by posterity, not the Enoch of chapter 4. Cain pleased his son, Enoch pleased God (Heb 11:5).

The line of Seth also recognised the *curse* (v. 29). As the fall is referred to in the early part of the chapter, so the curse is at the close. Now there is no word of the curse in chapter 4. Man in his natural state is not willing to notice nor to acknowledge the curse of God. Lamech in verse 29 certainly felt its weight and toil, and the awful blight it had left. Here is a wonderful experience that those of ch. 4 never dreamed of, that is "Prophecy", and the great hope it inspires in the breast of believers. Here in the prophecy of Lamech, the promise appears that the curse will one day be removed. When the Messiah shall come, the Lord Jesus, that righteous One, who has right to all the earth, He shall remove the curse during the *millennium* as clearly taught in Revelation 22:3. Perhaps the curse was a little relieved through Noah when he came into the new order of things after the flood. The complete removal awaits the golden age of the reign of Christ.

Now again as in the case of Enoch, contrasts can be

NOAH

drawn between the Lamech in chapter 4 and the one in chapter 5. There, Lamech appears as a poet, seeking to cover sin. Here another Lamech speaks as a prophet of the curse removed. The former boasts of what he will do, the latter of what another will do: Noah, and really the Lord. The name Lamech means "strength". He of chapter 4 boasts of himself, and fails to see he is only dust. The Lamech of chapter 5 admits the curse, "dust thou art and unto dust shalt thou return", and speaks of the strength of one to come, even the Lord Jesus.

Lamech was not alone in this prophecy. Enoch his grandfather also prophesied of the coming of the Lord according to the epistle of Jude, verse 14. So, darkness is the way of the men of chapter 4 while prophecy lights the way of the believers of chapter 5.

It is good to notice also the *progression* in the prophecies. Enoch spoke of the coming of the Lord and the resulting judgment; Lamech carries the prophecy forward to the millennial reign of Christ. Of course we know that all revelation is progressive, and here is an excellent example of this.

The godly of chapter 5 were very up to date in what they believed, and in keeping with the faith of God's people today. They believed as we do in:

1. the rest procured in the first advent of Christ, of which Noah and the ark were an excellent type.
2. the creation of all that is seen and unseen, including man.
3. the fall of man and the curse upon the earth because of sin.
4. the rapture of Enoch.
5. the Lord's coming in glory to judge the world and the ungodly.
6. headship in the man.
7. the coming millennium.

THE SPIRITUAL MAN OF GENESIS CHAPTER 5

Throughout the genealogy three names stand out, and further comments are made concerning them: Adam was blessed; Enoch walked with God; and Lamech looked forward to relief of the curse. These three beautifully link up with the well known division of Ephesians:

Chs. 1-3 the WEALTH of the believer, blessed in the heavenlies in Christ Jesus. So Adam was blessed and his headship was prominent, looking forward to Christ.

Chs. 4-5 the WALK of the believer; the word "walk" occurs five times, and in a different form each time. This of course links with Enoch who walked with God.

Ch. 6 the WARFARE of the believer, the whole armour, and the Word of the Spirit. This could be linked to Lamech who expresses having to battle with the curse, and then utters his word of prophecy by the Spirit.

Sad to say the evidence of fall is still here: man begins well but soon begins to degenerate. So here in the 600 years of the life of Noah the deterioration sets in, and corruption and violence fill the earth. Noah alone is acceptable to the Lord. However, this awaits chapter 6.

14

THE CORRUPT GENERATION OF GENESIS 6

A very simple structure will exhibit the main events of Genesis 6.

A. The corrupt earth, vv. 1-4
  B. God sees it, and plans its destruction, vv. 5-7
A. The righteous man, Noah, vv. 8-10
  B. God sees him, and plans his salvation, vv. 11-22.

During the six hundred years of Noah's life evil was really coming to a head, and much is said in few words at the beginning of the chapter. While the population increased so did the evil, and this is described in a twofold way: violence and corruption (vv. 11,12).

The violence would be directed towards man and the corruption largely towards God. While no doubt the descendants of Cain began the slide away from God those of the godly line soon came under the evil influence. In the final stages only Noah and his family were perfect in their generations. But something very sinister was at work also in the sons of God (v. 2). From this mingling of the sons of God with the daughters of men the corruption and violence escalated to such a degree that the judgment of the flood became necessary. This started with man doing his own will; note the close of v. 2: "they took them wives of all which they choose". When man is left to his own devices he always degenerates, and this has been manifested throughout the ages. It has often

THE CORRUPT GENERATION OF GENESIS 6

been said that God establishes things with man but soon deterioration sets in: from the perfect to the imperfect, from the spiritual to the fleshly. This is true, and can be traced in the spiritual history of man.

1. The beauty and blessing of Eden left in the hand of the man was soon destroyed by the wilful sin of him upon whom the responsibility rested, and God drove out the man.
2. Even Noah in chapter 9, after all the deliverance he experienced and the position he held, did some experimenting, became drunk, and brought a curse on some of his posterity. He abused the blessings of the new world.
3. Israel was called out of Egypt by the grace and power of God, but they soon disobeyed and fell as carcasses in the wilderness.
4. The priesthood with all its glory and beauty was soon corrupted by Nadab and Abihu, as they offered strange fire, and consequently suffered death by the discipline of the Lord.
5. Again, in the times of the Judges, great deliverances were wrought and the people rejoiced, but soon they went their sinful ways again, and so to further discipline. This circle of behaviour was repeated time and time again.
6. Also the grandeur of the kings, David and Solomon, and the temple filled with the glory of the Lord soon degenerated: the kings drifted into apostasy, the glory departed from the temple, the people were carried into captivity, and the gorgeous temple destroyed. Because of corruption and idolatry the land spewed them out of its mouth according to the warning of Leviticus 18:25.
7. Alas for the return from exile! A good beginning was

NOAH

made with the temple being rebuilt, but when Nehemiah came he found all in disarray and in careless carnality.
8. This last degenerated into religious bigotry without God that rejected and crucified the Lord of glory when He came to them.
9. Then the beautiful order of the New Testament churches soon fell into confusion and division, as church history manifests.
10. The perfection of the millennium, with its full prosperity and the curse removed, shall issue in a world wide revolt against God, and the fire of judgment becomes necessary.

Therefore we do not marvel that in the days of Noah, this degeneration continued inevitably towards the righteous judgment of the flood. The evil is summed up in the two words corruption and violence, which are mentioned together in verse 11. There is an expansion of each of these in the following verses. "And God looked upon the earth, and, behold, it was corrupt; for all flesh had corrupted his way upon the earth" (v. 12). Note the wording *his way*; they failed to walk in God's way, but sought out their own way and became as wandering sheep; the imagination and thoughts of the heart ruled the man. This was true of all flesh, Noah being the exception. Man had lowered himself to be beastly with no knowledge or thought of God. Isaiah 53:6 certainly sums up the man of those times: "All we like sheep have gone astray; we have turned everyone to his own way". The same principle is working in the natural man today; man is always the same.

The violence is then expanded in verse 13, "And God said unto Noah, The end of all flesh is come before me; for the earth is filled with violence through them; and,

THE CORRUPT GENERATION OF GENESIS 6

behold, I will destroy them with the earth". So man is the channel of all the violence upon the earth. All the wars, killings and hurtings throughout the ages have had their source in fallen man, with his envy, covetousness and lust for power. The beast of the jungle is today somewhat violent, it must have been more so in the dark days before the flood.

It is wonderful to see the absence of violence among the animals while they were in the ark, they could live in peace; no doubt it was a picture of the millennium.

Corruption is mainly before God, but it is also against self: "he that committeth fornication sinneth against his own body" (1 Cor 6:18). But violence is against our fellow men, taking away the rights of others by force, striking and hurting others; it issues out of a heart full of hatred. To sum up, corruption is really love of self, and violence comes out of hatred for others. The NT bears witness that the same features shall characterise the people of the last days: "men shall be lovers of their own selves" (2 Tim 3:2). The list goes on to describe the perilous times to come, and advances to "fierce, despisers of those that are good" (v.3). The word "fierce" stands out; this is the only place in the NT where it occurs; it means "wild, or savage". This certainly describes the violence that the Lord saw in that generation leading up to the flood. Man has always been so. According to 1 Timothy 1:9 the law "was made for... murderers of fathers, and murderers of mothers, for manslayers"; this is violence indeed. The next verse covers the other category of sin before the flood, corruption, identified as "whoremongers, for them that defile themselves with mankind". Again, it could be said that corruption is frequently practised in secret, whereas violence is very much in the public eye. Although when corruption is left unchecked it soon becomes public as is largely the case today.

NOAH

It is well known to Bible students that a trinity of evil heads up all sin under three chief categories: corruption, violence and falsehood, the latter covering all forms of idolatry. Now no hint of idolatry is seen in the days of Noah, but seems to emerge in Genesis 10 with Nimrod and Babylon. Abraham was certainly an idolater before the Lord of glory appeared to him (Jos 24:15). This shows that as the Lord progressively unfolds revelation and truth, so the powers of darkness gradually accelerate the progress of evil. It will be so until the end, "evil men and seducers shall wax worse and worse, deceiving, and being deceived"(2 Tim 3:13). And the mystery of iniquity is already at work according to 2 Thessalonians 2:7. This trinity of evil progresses to a climax in the three great personages of the last days, the violence of the beast, the falsehood of the false prophet, and the corruption of the scarlet woman (Rev 13 and 17).

Again, all three are seen at the cross, Judas sold the Lord for thirty pieces of silver which was an act of corruption, the Lord was falsely accused by Israel, and violently put to death by Rome.

Today, corruption is public news; people love to wallow in the mire of corruption which engulfs the great of this world in every sphere. Violence is everywhere, and we live in days when terrorism is the accepted thing. Falsehood is seen in the tremendous growth of the false cults of our day. Surely we are near the judgment, not by a flood but that by fire of which the apostle Peter speaks so vividly. We need to keep awake, and to be aware of the times.

15

THE SONS OF GOD

A problem confronts the student of Genesis 6 as he approaches the meaning of the term "the sons of God"; who are they? A lot depends on the answer, for if these be angels as many believe, it gives a real reason for the flood: it was necessary to cleanse away the poison that was coursing in the veins of the human race as a result of this unnatural union. Consider the passage. "And it came to pass, when men began to multiply on the face of the earth, and daughters were born unto them, That the sons of God saw the daughters of men that they were fair; and they took them wives of all which they choose". Then verse 4 teaches the outcome of this union, "There were giants in the earth in those days; and also after that, when the sons of God came in unto the daughters of men, and they bare children to them, the same became mighty men which were of old, men of renown".

Two schools of interpretation emerge here, one being, that the godless line of Cain (ch. 4) are the men who bear the daughters, and the sons of God belong to the godly line of Seth. The other idea is that these sons of God are angels, real angels that kept not their first estate and that it is to such that Jude refers in his epistle. Which of the two is right, and what does one believe? First, let us make a few Scriptural tests upon the idea that the sons are the godly line of Seth, and the daughters are of the ungodly descendants of Cain.

NOAH

"Sons of God" is a term that is never used of mankind in the Old Testament unless of course this is the meaning here. Such a title seems to have awaited the coming of Christ, and the experience of the new birth that comes by faith in Him. True, Adam is called a son of God in Luke 3, but this is peculiar to him alone, as he came by actual creation from the fingers of God, whereas the rest of humanity came into this world by natural birth. Now that God has revealed Himself in grace through the first advent of Christ, sonship is a grand reality; believers are made the sons of God as they are linked to the Lord by faith. Three classic passages in the NT deal with the sonship of the believer, the first being Ephesians 1, where sonship is traced from the past eternal purposes of God, and now made real in Christ. Romans 8 looks into the future and sees the manifestation of the sons of God when the Lord shall appear in glory at His second advent. Galatians 4, the third passage, considers sonship as a present reality and blessing, and the moral implications that issue from such a position before the Lord. But all this is NT revelation.

The word that is used for men in verse 1 is the Hebrew word *adam* used in 1:26: "Let us make man in our image": so it may mean the first man Adam. Chapter 5:2 is the same: "God...called their name Adam", or man. Later the word came to be used of the posterity of the first man being of course all that sprang of him. There is the possibility that the man of chapter 6:1 is Adam himself, and that the daughters are his, as verse 4 of chapter 5 says of Adam, "he begat sons and daughters". If this be so (and "man" is singular), then the event happened early in human history, and had developed until the days of Noah.

Again if the word "men" means the descendants of Adam, being his sons, then "the daughters of men" are

THE SONS OF GOD

the daughters of mankind without distinction.

Throughout the chapter "man" and "men" are used of all humanity without distinction: "God saw that the wickedness of man was great in the earth" (v. 5); "it repented the Lord that he had made man" (v. 6); "the Lord said, I will destroy man whom I have created" (v. 7). (See JND on 6:1).

Why should the union of believers with unbelievers produce such marvellous children?. The unequal yoke today does no such thing. Christian marriages, marriages between unbelievers and believers, and between unsaved persons produce similar offspring. If it was otherwise before the flood, why is it not so now? mankind has not changed and the effects of the fall are still present although man is much better informed.

There was obviously a progression in this evil; it started when men began to multiply upon the earth (v. 1), and continued up to the five hundredth. year of the life of Noah, when the mind of the Lord was made known. So it was a gradual thing; first some defected, then others followed in the unholy union, until only the family of Noah was left untouched.

Now consider the other school of thought, namely, that these sons of God were angels. The Scripture seems to lean in that direction, although many things are necessarily difficult to explain.

Angels are definitely called the sons of God in three different passages:

1. Job 1:6, where a look into the spirit world is afforded to the reader; the curtains of heavenly scenes are drawn back as the sons of God come to present themselves to God. These are stewards and are giving an account of their responsibilities. This is not unique as the same thought occurs in Zechariah 1:10-11, the

angel is giving a report before the Lord. Again in Zechariah 6:1-8 the vision of chariots and horses is certainly a look into the spirit world.
2. Job 2:1 is a similar event, and needs no comment.
3. Job 38:7, speaking of the creation, "the morning stars sang together, and all the sons of God shouted for joy". In the context the stars are the angels, and the sons of God are the same. (Those that love the poetic books of the Bible will know that an idea is repeated twice, and sometimes three times in different forms; such is the case here).

God had an audience when He created the earth, an audience that appreciated His wonderful power and wisdom, namely the angels. Angels also admired the great heavenly movement of the Lord Jesus becoming incarnate (Luke 2:9-14). The comment upon this in 1Tim 3:16 is: "seen of angels". Again, in Luke 15 the angels express an appreciation of the grace that saves a sinner, God's power is at work again, but with the wonderful added grace.

Now to be consistent, if the sons of God in Job 38 are angels, why should they not be angels in Genesis 6 also? On the other hand the title sons of God is never applied to men in the OT. It is used in the NT in the following three ways:

1. Adam was the son of God (Luke 3:38), but this was by direct creation as he was not born of parents. Again, it is well to remember that "son" is in italics, and not in the original Scriptures; what it really says is "Adam, which was of God" (see JND).
2. The Lord is eternally Son of God as being divine (Luke 1:35; Matt 16; John 1:49); such expressions as "the only begotten Son" are used of the Lord, and of no one else.

THE SONS OF GOD

3. Believers are sons of God by redemption (Rom 8:19). Ordinary men, even believers in OT days were the people of God, they were never called sons of God. This heavenly position awaited the coming of redemption; through the work of Christ it is now true of all believers.

This falling away of angels in Genesis 6 explains the apostasy of angels spoken of by Jude, "The angels that kept not their first estate". The RV renders this, "their proper estate". They had a position but left it for another. It seems to the writer that Jude was speaking directly of the sons of God in the passage under consideration.

Angels are spirits (Heb 1:14) and cannot be seen by the natural man. When they are sent to earth with a message for men they come in the form of a man. They were not born men as was our Lord, but rather were made to possess a body for a limited time. Such was the case in Genesis 18, where three men appeared to Abraham. One was the Lord, the other two were angels. Again in chapter 19 two men came to Lot with a mission, but the wicked men of the city of Sodom were intent on committing sodomy with them; they saw them as men not as angels. The angels there *kept their first estate* and judged the men of the city with blindness, and later with the fire and brimstone. Now in chapter 6 the sons of God being angels were upon the earth for a purpose; they had a mission of which we know nothing. These angels having bodies of men were attracted to women and so fell; *they kept not their first estate.* They desired to remain men and to indulge in the lusts of the flesh rather than to be the servants of God in angel form.

This is in keeping with the context of Jude who is speaking of lust that results in apostasy: Israel lusted after Egypt in the wilderness; these fallen angels lusted after women; and Sodom lusted after strange flesh. The order is significant: Israel is mentioned first, although last chronologically, because unbelief is the first step. This is followed by apostasy in the angels, apostasy being the outcome of persistent unbelief. Finally Sodom and Gomorrah which manifested the things that accompany a reprobate mind (Rom 1:28). The order is moral. If one persists in unbelief he eventually gives up God which is apostasy, then God gives him over to a reprobate mind. This was the condition of Sodom.

An objection to this interpretation is often raised based on Matthew 22 where the Lord, speaking of the resurrection, points out that those raised from the dead do not marry but are like the angels in heaven (v.30), thus teaching that angels are sexless. But a careful reading resolves the difficulty, "the angels ... in heaven" not on earth. The sons of God of in Genesis 6 were not in heaven but on the earth with bodies, and yielded to temptation. The two angels that stood by the tomb of the risen Lord were not in heaven then, and were seen as two men (Luke 24:4).

The strange outcome of the union was significant: the children born were "mighty men which were of old, men of renown". Their might no doubt led to the violence that filled the earth. Renown describes their extraordinary exploits; infamy would be a better word. These were in addition to the giants that existed, so making the world a terrible place.

But what is meant by "of old" (v.4)? It would seem that this is a reference to the previous existence of the angels who passed on something of their nature to this devilish offspring. Similar things will happen when the days of Daniel 2 and Revelation 8 and 9 are fulfilled upon the earth.

Because of this unholy union it is not surprising to

THE SONS OF GOD

read of the terrible violence and the accompanying corruption. Behind it all was the serpent. God had promised that the seed of the woman would crush the serpents head (Gen 3:15), and from that time the serpent was against the seed of the woman (that is Christ) seeking in some manner to destroy or corrupt the royal seed. Such was the case of Athaliah who killed, as she thought, all the king's sons (2 Chron 22), but God saw to it that Joash escaped, and the royal seed was preserved. The storm on the sea while the Lord was asleep in the boat was another effort of the devil, and many such references could be added. Really this is what is seen here in Genesis 6. It is an attempt by the serpent to pollute the seed of the woman. The epistle to the Hebrews especially presses home the fact that the Lord was a man in all points like ourselves apart from sin. This then was the reason for the flood: to wipe out that polluted generation, and to start again in Noah. He and his family alone were untainted by this corruption of blood. Today there is violence and corruption upon the earth on a scale equal to if not greater than in Noah's day, yet no flood nor similar judgment has resulted. The reason is simply that the same conditions do not exist, and the Messiah has come. Man is vile and God will eventually judge him in a final way, but this case was vastly different.

The giants were not produced by the devilish union. Two classes are noticed, separated by the word "also". The giants *(nephilim* is the word used here and in Numbers 13:33 of the giants in Canaan) are mentioned first. Then comes the word "also", and the story of the sons of God, classing the seed of the sons of God in a different category from the giants. These giants appear later in the history of Israel; they will always remember Og king of Bashan and especially Goliath of Gath. The Nephilim, as they were called, had to be destroyed by

NOAH

the sword of Israel at the commandment of the Lord. So these, being upon the earth at the same time as the angels and their terrible offspring, added to the violent state of the then world.

Finally, the words that describe Noah are enlightening; he "was perfect in his generations". The word "perfect" that is used here is the same as that used of the paschal lamb of the passover: without blemish. So Noah was physically as well as morally right in the eyes of the Lord. All the rest of his generation were in some way affected by the angel union as described.

The attempt by man to be equal with God first appeared in Genesis 3: "ye shall be as gods". The fall was the result. Here is another attempt; it ended with the flood. Babel of chapter 11 was a further attempt, and ended with confusion. Man is allowed by God to subdue the earth and have dominion over it, but God always frustrates his feeble efforts to be equal with Him.

16

*THE EVIL GENERATION
OF GENESIS 6 - 8*

The Lord in His ministry made reference to the days of Noah in Luke 17 and in Matthew 24. In both these the prime point the Lord makes is the careless attitude of the people towards God, and their blindness to the fact of impending judgment. The record itself is found in Genesis 6-8, and covers the history of those generations in few words.

As well as the impure offspring of the sons of God, giants were present on the earth at the same time. These were not the result of the unholy union of angels, but were in addition to that evil. These giants were anything but attractive, and appeared again in Canaan when the people sought to enter the land in Numbers 13, and again in the days of Joshua. They had various names: "the nephilim" which is the word used in Genesis 6:4; the "the Anakims" (Deut 2:11), no doubt the same sons of Anak as are mentioned in Numbers 13:33; and the "Rephaim" (Deut 2:20), whom the Ammonites call "Zamzummins". Where they came from or who they were is not made clear. The Lord intends that saints should see the spiritual import. They are pictures of the flesh, and the command of the Lord was that they should be "utterly destroyed". The believer is commanded to do the same thing in Romans 8:13, that is, to put to death the deeds of the body, which is the outlet for the works of the flesh. If Israel had not killed the giants, the giants

NOAH

would soon have slaughtered puny Israel; so Romans warns, "If ye live after the flesh ye shall die", that is, your spiritual life will be wasted. A giant is an overgrowth of the flesh, attractive to the natural man who looks for the best that man can produce, but no giants ever came of the posterity of Israel. Again, there is no record of a giant turning to God in Scripture; they remained enemies of the Lord and of His people.

Verses 5 and 6 are most interesting, the first being a disclosure of the heart of man: "every imagination of the thought of his heart", and the other of the heart of God: "it grieved him at his heart".

"It repented the Lord that he had made man" (v. 6). The same thought occurs again in 1 Samual 15:11, "It repenteth me that I have set up Saul to be king", And in 2 Samuel 24:16, "And when the angel stretched out his hand upon Jerusalem, to destroy it, the Lord repented him of the evil". This is very difficult when the opposite is clearly stated in Numbers 23:19, "God is not a man, that he should lie; neither the son of man, that he should repent: hath he said, and shall he not do it? or hath he spoken, and shall he not make it good?" How can these differences be reconciled?. The difference between the purposes of God and His ways must be clearly understood.

The purposes of God cannot be set aside, and are as sure as the eternal throne, but the ways of God are variable, and can be altered according to how they are received by responsible man. The best illustration of this is found in the words of the Lord to Moses at the burning bush: "I am come down to deliver them (Israel) out of the hand of the Egyptians, and to bring them up out of that land unto a good land and a large, unto a land flowing with milk and honey (Exod 3:8). Now there was no mention of the wilderness, yet that took up forty

THE EVIL GENERATION OF GENESIS 6 - 8

years of their lives. The wilderness was *the ways of God*, and the promised land was *the purposes of God*. The ways of God are clearly seen in Deuteronomy 8:2, "thou shalt remember *all the way* which the Lord thy God led thee these forty years in the wilderness, to humble thee, and to prove thee, to know what was in thine heart, whether thou wouldest keep his commandments, or no".

When this difference is understood, the difficulty in the Lord repenting fades away. In Numbers 23 God was speaking of His fixed purpose for the nation of Israel, as the context clearly shows. He cannot repent or go back on those purposes; the gifts and calling of God are without repentance (Rom 11:29).

The other passages have to do with the trying of man in responsibility and therefore with the ways of God. If the man fails, God can repent of what He would have done for them in blessing.

Although "it repented the Lord that he had made man" this did not set aside the eternal purposes of God. Nothing was hindered by the flood, a Man shall yet reign in righteousness over the works of His hands and we shall reign with Him.

The other statement is very far reaching: "it grieved him at his heart". Man's attitude and behaviour can affect the heart of God. It is certainly true that God can affect the hearts of men, but the reverse is seldom reckoned with. The perfect man Christ Jesus was the cause of heaven being opened and the deep pleasure of God fully expressed. Romans 14:6-8 teaches that no man liveth unto himself: but unto the Lord, we affect Him by our lives.

How wonderful it is to think that the saint can bring pleasure to his Lord by sincerity, sanctification, obedience, and in all the service rendered in His Name.

121

NOAH

But the opposite is also true, we can grieve Him, just as we can grieve the Holy Spirit (Eph 4:30). To God the saints are the salt of the earth. God has no pleasure in anything else on this doomed earth. The saints are so insignificant among the seemingly great of the land, yet they can delight the heart of the eternal God in glory. In Genesis 6 God was grieved in His heart because of the way His creation had gone, the unholy alliances, the violence and corruption; now He must destroy it.

There is also a double statement describing the ways of man, which give the reason for the grief found in the heart of the Lord in verse 6.

"God saw that the wickedness of man was great in the earth" (v.5). Here is the fruit of the fall and of the evil canker of verse 2. All is manifest and nothing can be hidden from the eyes of the Lord. The people seemed to be without shame and Noah likely denounced uncompromisingly the evils practised so openly in his day. It is the duty of Christians to do the same today. They are the only light the world now has, and the child of the Lord ought to speak out against the evil that is practised. Note the wording here: "*the wickedness of man*" not of men. The fallen nature of all men is in view. From the fall of the first man, Adam, all have been as he was. People like to think they have a divine spark, but man, the total man is wicked and sinful: he cannot cease from sin.

The root is also seen: "Every imagination of the thoughts of his heart was only evil continually". To this must be added the endorsement in chapter 8:21, "For the imagination of man's heart is evil from his youth". All men are included as the word "man" indicates. Every imagination of the thoughts means that the natural mind is contrary to God in every possible way. The Lord implies this in Isaiah 55:8-9, "For my thoughts are not your thoughts, neither are your ways my ways saith the

THE EVIL GENERATION OF GENESIS 6 - 8

Lord". The imagination of the heart can be well understood from Paul's comprehensive description of the natural man in Ephesians 2:2-3. "Wherein in time past you walked according to the course of this world, according to the prince of the power of the air, the spirit that now worketh in the children of disobedience: Among whom also we all had our conversion in times past in the lusts of our flesh, fulfilling the desires of the flesh and of the *mind*". The imagination of the heart is the same as the desires of the mind. The things they wanted to do and intended to do, they did, without considering God, and more often in defiance of the ways of God.

This sheds light on the word "repentance" which means a change of mind, seeking no longer one's own way but the way of the Lord, judging one's self to be guilty in the sight of a holy God.

In 8:21, after the flood was over the Lord said, "the imagination of man's heart is evil from his youth". This means that the cause for the flood was not merely the evil imagination of the heart of man, but something more sinister, even the unnatural alliance between the angelic sons of God and the daughters of men. The heart of man in just the same, but no further flood is necessary.

Another point to be observed in this verse, is that God counts our youthful years as years of responsibility. He does not say from birth, while all are sinners from birth, but from youth, the early age at which he goes astray from the teaching of God following the imagination and thoughts of the natural heart. The long list of sins and crimes in Romans 1 describes man after the flood, so man did not change. The flood brought about geographical changes but none in the heart of man.

Every imagination is affected, not only some, but all. The man, totally depraved, is set aside as guilty before God. Man does not want any restraint from God or any

NOAH

other authority, but will wax worse. Iniquity will abound until the Lord comes to put an end to all of man's foolish imagination.

Noah was one hundred years in building the ark, and all that time the evil was increasing. At the same time Noah was preaching righteousness and the long suffering of the Lord waited. They likely thought he was a fool, building a boat on dry land and the nearest water many miles away.

"God speaketh once, yea twice yet man perceiveth it not". God spoke to the people in at least three ways during those days.

1. There was a righteous testimony in both the life of Noah and in his preaching, but men love darkness rather than light because their deeds are evil, so this was rejected.
2. The building of the ark was a sign, something they could see; this also went unheeded by all the people. Signs are seldom recognised. In the Gospels the people asked for a sign, yet the Lord was multiplying them every day.
3. The terrible increase of sin was also a message: "Where will it all end?" ought to have been in the minds of the people, rather than their sole occupation with their intents of the heart to do evil.

Now all three voices are in the world today: the testimony of the gospel and the lives of the Christians, so different from those of the world.

The signs in Israel and the nations and the terrible increase in every form of evil indicate that the coming of the Lord is near. People ought to be thinking, and repenting, but as it was in the days of Noah, so is the world of our day.

THE EVIL GENERATION OF GENESIS 6 - 8

Chapter 7 treats of the flood, water gushing out suddenly from above and from beneath; it must have come as a great shock to the people. The only place of safety was in the ark, but the door was shut by God Himself and entry was impossible. There was no hope, nothing but despair and remorse, then a watery grave, and into eternal darkness. They found no place of repentance although perhaps some sought it carefully with tears. Such was the inglorious end of the generation that forgot God, who rejected all the light that the Lord gave them, who choose to follow the evil intent of their own hearts. All this will be repeated on a greater scale when the Lord returns. However, it is of the similar careless attitude that the Lord warns the generation immediately prior to His coming again.

The raven in chapter 8 left the ark and did not return. It was content with a world under judgment, a picture again of the natural man, unclean as the raven. It found its congenial environment in the carcasses floating upon the waters of judgment.

So all that man was, all his glory, and the glory of that great civilisation sank beneath the waves of that judgment flood. They were people great in progress and business but great in sin as well, and mixing in unholy alliances. These demanded the judgment of God for the preservation of the race of man, and for the eventual securing of His purpose in the perfect Man, Christ Jesus, and His righteous reign over all the works of His hands.

17

A PASSAGE IN JOB

An interesting passage from the book of Job must be considered as having a bearing upon the generation before the flood, namely Job 21:7-18.

Job is known to be a very early book, and it could well be that this is a direct reference to the indifference of the people to the Lord, and to the preaching of Noah in his day. It proves to be a wonderful treatise on a generation that had completely turned away from God in the face of impending judgment, and describes exactly the case of the antediluvians. It fits the picture so well that if it is not a direct reference, it can certainly be applied with great profit.

Here is the passage.

> "Wherefore do the wicked live, become old, yea, are mighty in power?
> Their seed is established in their sight with them, and their offspring before their eyes.
> Their houses are safe from fear, neither is the rod of God upon them.
> Their bull gendereth, and faileth not; their cow calveth, and casteth not her calf.
> They send forth their little ones like a flock, and their children dance.
> They take the timbrel and harp, and rejoice at the sound of the organ.
> They spend their days in wealth, and in a moment go down to the grave.

Therefore they say unto God, Depart from us; for we desire not the knowledge of thy ways.

What is the Almighty, that we should serve him? and what profit should we have, if we pray unto him?

Lo, their good is not in their hand: the counsel of the wicked is far from me.

How oft is the candle of the wicked put out? and how oft cometh their destruction upon them? God distributeth sorrows in his anger.

They are as stubble before the wind, and are as chaff that the storm carrieth away".

The passage covers the independent and indifferent state of the people in a fivefold way.

They lived to a good old age in (v. 7), which the antedeluvians certainly did, as is evident from Genesis 5.

They waxed mighty in power, a reference perhaps to the mighty men and the giants of chapter 6. Their houses are safe from fear, neither is the rod of God upon them, which was true of the long suffering of God as He waited in the days of Noah.

Family life appears in vv. 8-11; families that increase and have plenty, whose seed is established in their sight with them, the family business passing to the sons and grandsons. They are also well cared for: little ones go forth as a well cared for flock, and learn to dance with joy. It all seems to be so happy, yet they live without God.

The children engage in the dance to the delight and amusement of parents. Others find pleasure in the timbrel and harp, and rejoice at the sound of the organ. All this issued from the inventions of Tubalcain (see ch. 4).

The bull gendereth and faileth not, their cows calf and none are still born; all are in perfect health, which prospers the farmer no doubt. They spend their days in wealth is the clear statement of v. 13, that really means the possessions, and enjoyment of things that wealth can produce. Such was the case in Genesis 4: possessions are prominent. They were occupied with the temporal and not with the eternal (2 Cor 4:18).

Often to such prosperity people add a little religious savour to ease the conscience of the extravagant living, and to put up a show of respectability. But not so here; they say to God, "Depart from us". This was the attitude of the unclean demon in the man, causing him to cry to the Lord, "leave us alone" (Mark 1:30), and of those who had lost the herds of swine who besought the Lord to depart from them (Mark 5). They desired not the knowledge of the ways of the Lord (v.14), each as a wandering sheep had turned to his own way.

Their arrogance is manifested in the statement, "What is the Almighty that we should serve him?", not, Who is he? rather, What is He? as if His ways were but an influence. They did not even pray to the Lord; certainly He was forgotten, and a terrible independence of the Creator was the order of the day. This was a negative response to the long suffering of the Lord and to the faithful preaching of Noah, yet those days were a visitation of grace and of the Spirit, as Peter informs us in 1 Peter 3. In spite of the Spirit's movement, the people loved their sinful ways and thought that all things would continue as they had from the beginning of the creation. The answer of God to their indifference was the sudden flood that took them all away.

The next verses describe this; God distributed sorrows in His anger. They were as stubble before the wind, as chaff that the wind carries away. This is exactly what happened; and it all fits so well.

How often this is the case. The days of Jeremiah are an example: Ezekiel was preaching as well as he, warning of the imminent fall of the city of Jerusalem. The Spirit was there, but the response was negative. The enemy was at the gates, sins were mounting, then sudden destruction came and the city fell under the wrath of the Lord. Soon this will be repeated in the days prior to the day of the Lord: they will say, Peace, peace; then sudden destruction shall come, and they shall not escape (1 Thess 5:3).

This passage in Job, then, gives a searching commentary on the attitude of the people just before the flood burst forth and took them all away, but the purpose and grace of the Lord saw to the saving of the eight souls by means of the ark.

The next consideration will be the man Noah himself, the exercise and character that he manifested. This will prove to be a subject sweeter by far than what has engaged the reader in the character of the generation that fell under the judgment of the flood.

18

NOAH, THE MAN

Noah was a most remarkable man yet he does not get the place of interest among Christians that he deserves. Really he is one of the great men in the word of God. The fact that the New Testament writers refer to him so often is proof of this. He bore testimony in the most shockingly wicked days, surrounded by terrible evil and moral pollution yet he went on for God for over five hundred years. To go on faithfully is something to be desired by every one that loves the Lord, although we cannot live as long as he. The passage says, "Noah was a just man, and perfect in his generations, and Noah walked with God" (Gen 6:9). Again,"Thee have I seen righteous before me in this generation" (7:1).

As we consider his record in the four chapters of Genesis we see a very versatile man indeed.

He is called by Peter "a *preacher* of righteousness". In spite of a very busy life he found time to preach. We can be assured that he put his all into his messages and his preaching. A good message, skilfully and sincerely set before the people was his continual faithful witness no doubt. He would be instant in season and out of season, as Paul exhorted Timothy. Nor was he discouraged at the lack of response to his tidings; patiently he went on with the job, knowing he was doing the will of God. He had a great satisfaction in this, besides leaving the people without excuse.

NOAH, THE MAN

He is distinguished also by building, first the ark and later the altar, so he could well be called a *builder*. Paul speaks of builders in 1 Corinthians 3; he was a builder himself: he laid foundations and sought to build up assemblies and the people of God; he encourages others to build also, but teaches that it is a great responsibility to build and that those who do so should take great care. What a pity it is if all the labour that goes into building is lost by the edifice falling down because of faulty material or workmanship. Noah's work of building the ark stood the test of the severest conditions. Would that we all could build like this man.

It can be added to this that he was *skilful*. It took great skill to follow the pattern of the structure given by God: to set out the foundation or framework, to balance and to strengthen so as to resist the waves. If we had seen the finished work we would have marvelled at the workmanship. Skill was needed later in the building of the altar, but even more so in the discernment of what was clean and what was unclean among the animals. This was the more remarkable as there was as yet no direction from the Lord. Leviticus 11, which has to do with the clean and unclean, had not been written as yet.

In 1 Corinthians 3 Paul urges this skill in assembly building, in giving the ministry that the Lord will use and that will refresh and build up the saints. He solemnly warns, "let every man take heed how he buildeth" on the foundation that he has laid. The Corinthians were building with the flesh and not with the Spirit; they were busy building into the believers the wisdom of the world and not the wisdom taught by the Holy Spirit. Really they were babes and not full grown to maturity in divine truths. The writer to the Hebrews goes to the heart of the matter with the words, "For every one that useth milk is unskilful in the word of righteousness: for he is a babe"(5:13). By milk he means childish ministry that cannot bring the saints to a fuller understanding of the grace wherein they stand. This skill comes only from training in the school of God: the man with the Word, and the appetite for it, his teacher being the Holy Spirit. The willingness to take the time to study will soon develop and one becomes skilful in the word of righteousness.

"Milk" and "meat" are used both in 1 Corinthians 3 and Hebrews 5 to indicate the simple truths so necessary to the young believer, and the deeper things that God would have us enjoy. In the early stages of Christian life we need the milk as we know so little (1 Pet 2:2), but it is the purpose of God to bring the student to maturity that the meat of the Word may be enjoyed.

However, there is a sad contrast between the two passages: while in 1 Corinthians 3:1-4 the incident that brings forth the rebuke of Paul is the lack of growth, in Hebrews 5 they had grown but fell back, "When for the time ye ought to be teachers, ye have need that one teach you again which be the first principles of the oracles of God". For the Corinthians time had gone on, they had had the best of teachers, yet they were still in the milk stage of the understanding of divine things. However the warning to the Hebrews was more serious still. It was a sad condition and a warning to all. Knowledge of the Word can be lost and, if one does not go on in the things of the Lord, and seek to grow, he then goes back. The Lord spoke about this condition in a parable: "For unto every one that hath shall be given, and he shall have abundance: but from him that hath not shall be taken away even that which he hath" (Matt 25:29). So the principle remains: the student must keep up the study of the Word. The Bible is a big volume, and one can soon forget much of its contents unless study is steadily maintained. Not only so, but the people who listen to the ministry of such will soon detect a staleness in the messages.

From the consideration of these things it is evident that Noah was an *active* man. The Lord was very active, so were the apostles, and basic Christianity is doing as well as talking. "If ye know these things, happy are ye if ye do them", are the words of the Lord in John 13:17. He Himself is the great example of this: "all that Jesus began to do and teach", is how Luke describes the ministry of our Lord (Acts 1:1). Also, the two disciples on the road to Emmaus spoke of Him as "a man mighty in deed and word" (Luke 24:19). In the Gospel record often this is the sequence in which our Lord operated. For example in John 6 He fed the hungry people with the few loaves and fishes then preached the sermon on the bread of life. Again, in chapter 8 He gave sight to the blind man then He proceeded to preach that He was the Light of the world. Love is expressed in action, and this is the character of Christianity; His disciples must not only preach the gospel, but love one another as well.

He was also a *family man*, and in spite of such a busy active life he was able to care and influence them. He had a wife and three sons, and daughters in law. How often the servant of the Lord is hindered by family responsibilities, and many make it an excuse for slothfulness, and blame much failure on their children or their partner in life. Adam was the first to do this, and men have been doing it since. "The woman whom thou gavest to be with me, she gave me of the tree, and I did eat", were his words, and so sought to blame his wife for his failure. The family did not stand in the way of Noah; he was head of the house, and the names of neither his wife nor his son's wives are left on record. No doubt he had busy times with the household, and being a very active man he would not shirk from any responsibility. Besides he was able to bring his sons with him into the ark. Neither Lot, nor Eli nor Samuel, nor even David to a large extent was able to influence his family. So we must admire Noah in this also. He was a family man, but this was not allowed to hinder him in his walk and service for the Lord.

He was an *obedient man*. This is one of his strongest points, as obedience has great priority with God: "to obey is better than sacrifice, and to hearken than the fat of rams" (1 Sam 15:22); "If ye love me, keep my commandments" (John 14:15). Noah's obedience is much marked in the Genesis record: "Thus did Noah; according to all that God commanded him" (Gen 6:22); "And Noah did according unto all that the Lord commanded him" (Gen 7:5); "There went in two and two unto Noah into the ark, the male and the female, as God had commanded Noah" (Gen 7:9); "they that went in, went in male and female of all flesh, as God had commanded him" (Gen 7:16); "God spake unto Noah, saying, Go forth of the ark, ... and Noah went forth" (Gen 8:16-18). Noah did all that the Lord commanded him, and this was very pleasing to the Lord. Obedience to the call of the gospel is the first great blessing to man. Salvation is obtained by obeying from the heart that form of doctrine which has been delivered us. This was the happy experience of the saints in Rome.

But it did not stop there as Romans 6 teaches; they were to go on to obey the Lord in the Christian life. The passage is binding on all believers, "Know ye not, that to whom ye yield yourselves servants to obey, his servants ye are to whom ye obey; whither of sin unto death, or obedience unto righteousness" (Rom 6:16-17). So obedience was paramount in the life of Noah, and should be in that of every believer.

Again, he must have been a very *patient man*. His patience in the building of the ark must be taken into account. It must have been very tedious work as he had no modern tools. Each plank had to be cut out, planed and measured; each nail had to be made. He must have seen very little result from months of work, but on he went little by little, plank by plank perhaps months apart in construction. He must have been patient also in preaching, as he was busily engaged in preaching righteousness for many years with no response. He did not give up after a few weeks or even months, nor does he seem to have questioned the point in preaching. On he went patiently, right to the day he entered the ark. He was willing to wait God's time, a thing which many of the great men in the Bible failed to do. Moses was not willing to wait; he thought the time had come for him to deliver Israel. In fact he was forty years too soon (Exod 2,3). David sought to build a house for the Lord (2 Sam 7); he too was premature; his son Solomon was to build a house of the Lord. Saul could not wait until Samuel came, and forced himself to offer to the Lord, and so lost the kingdom (1 Sam 13). This is a common failure even with the saintliest of men, and the examples of this can be traced throughout the Word. It is a most difficult thing to be patient; it certainly is against human nature. People love to see results, to obtain things quickly. However, Noah was marked by this patience which is so acceptable to the Lord.

The example of the Lord Jesus in this is seen in many parts of the prophetic Word, and was certainly seen in His ministry. This is hinted at in 2 Thess 3:5, "The Lord direct your hearts into the love of God, and into the patient waiting for Christ". The RV renders the last phrase "into the patience of Christ". Therefore, it is not a reference to His coming but to His character. He so

NOAH

beautifully displayed upon the earth that He was patient. No matter what happened, He committed Himself into the love of God for Him, and knew that God His Father would eventually bring all things into subjection to His own will. The saints now are patiently waiting for His return. Noah was a wonderful example of all this: he could await God's time, and certainly occupied until the judgment fell.

It seems he was also a *farmer,* as is learned later from his planting of a vineyard. It was likely beyond him to buy the amount of food that was needed for so many animal creatures in the ark, and for such a long period. Besides, he would hardly have bought from the ungodly. Perhaps he put his farming ability to work, and grew abundantly all that was necessary. Again, it is a farmer's work to care for livestock, and he had plenty of that with him in the ark.

We could also say that in a certain sense he was a *zoologist.* No zoo today has the variety of animals that Noah had with him in the ark. He had to care for them, feed them, keep their stalls clean, and all the difficult work that the keeping of animals entails. There were wild creatures and domesticated animals together in the one ark. This is what fascinates children about the ark: the thought of lions and other wild beasts all subdued and cared for by Noah.

Not only did he build the ark, he built also an altar; indeed he is the first one in the Bible recorded as having done so: "And Noah builded an altar unto the Lord" (8:20). Now as this was original, and no previous instruction had been given, the skill of the man is evident. He knew what would please the Lord, for the Lord smelled a sweet savour from that altar. Later a very detailed pattern for the altar of burnt offering in the tabernacle was given, and Moses was warned that all had

NOAH, THE MAN

to be made according to that pattern shown him in the mount. So we can see the wisdom of Noah. The altar must have been simple but effective, as the result of his offering was far reaching, securing the future of the earth, and being linked with the promises and the great Noahic covenant.

He thus functioned as a *priest*. He offered; he was a worshipper of the only true God. His worship was greatly accepted by the Lord: "And the Lord smelled a sweet savour, and the Lord said in his heart, I will not again curse the ground any more for man's sake" (8:21). So it was a worship that really reached to the heart of the Lord, and was received. In a later dispensation a priest required to be a very skilful man in the law and the tabernacle service, and had to be familiar with the different offerings and the inwards of those sacrifices, besides all the different feasts that were held throughout the Jewish Year. Noah's ritual was less complex but he was a priest just the same. There can be priestly service only when the Lord has given revelation of Himself, as seen in all the details of the law and the tabernacle given to Moses. So also here there was revelation: that of the coming flood; the detailed instruction for the building of the ark; and the covenant made with the Lord and Noah.

Moreover he was a *spiritual* man, a man of discernment, one who could appreciate exactly what the Lord required. This is the real meaning of spiritual; a spiritual person is one who can enter into the things that God delights in. This intelligent approach to God is unknown to the natural man who has no conception of what pleases the Lord nor what is required of him. Noah's spirituality is seen in his ability to distinguish between the clean and the unclean. How did he know the difference? He seemingly was not instructed in the past, it was just his spiritual intuition beautifully coming

137

NOAH

out. This subject will arise later in the study.

Next we see him as a vinedresser. He began to plant, he became an *husbandman*, or one who plants a vineyard. He was old by now; he had accomplished so much in life, but still he was looking for things to do. It is interesting to know that this is the first mention of vines and wine in the Word of God and it resulted in a curse upon Canaan. It has often been pointed out that the first mention of bread was in connection with the curse in Genesis 3. But the first time we get these two together it turns out to be a blessing: Abraham met Melchizedek, who gave him bread and wine, and blessed him.

But a sad word could be added to his list of great achievements: he was a *sleeping man*. It would seem the vineyard was to give him an interest in his old age, but it became a snare to him, and he was found drunken and sleeping. It is recorded of Samuel that he was sleeping before his great exploits began, before he knew the Lord, but never after. "Awake thou that sleepest...and Christ shall give thee light" (Eph 5:14). "They that sleep, sleep in the night; and they that be drunken, are drunken in the night", is the word of 1 Thess 5:7, and both these things were true of Noah in the last of his experiences on record in the Book of Genesis. How sad it is that one who ran so well ended so badly, and was the means of bringing a curse upon his family. It is always good to start well, it is excellent to continue well, but it is blessed to end well. Unfortunately, Noah did not. This sadly is a common occurrence in Scripture; we could think of Samson, Solomon, Gideon, Jephthah and others. All are beacons of warning to the saints of God. The old nature is still with us, and life can take so many twists and turns that seem to unsettle us, bringing out that which we did not realize was in our hearts. So the story ends with a solemn warning.

19

THE GODLY MAN

It will be profitable to consider in a little more detail some of the remarks already made concerning this wonderful man. We shall focus on four facets that will fully set forth this remarkable life, consider him as:

1. an *energetic* man;
2. a *godly* man;
3. a *priestly* man;
4. a *man of like passions* with ourselves

Noah was very much *the energetic man.* He was always busily occupied, and never shirked a task regardless how daunting. He built the ark apparently single handed as there is no mention of his sons helping, or of hired labour. Most would have considered the task of building a boat 450 feet long, three stories high and 75 feet broad, totally impossible, but not so Noah. He must have laboured hard year in and year out. Imagine the toil and sweat, working from the early morning to the late hours of the evening. It would seem that he did not know exactly when the flood would occur, so he was constantly racing against time. Many a problem must have been encountered, yet he patiently thought it out and started working again. Besides this he gathered and stored food, most likely growing it himself as suggested earlier; this too was a enormous task. We have only a faint idea of how many animals were in the shelter of that ark; what food must it have taken to satisfy the appetites of all for about a year or so. The task was great, but no murmur seems to have fallen from the lips of this man; he had the energy to get on with the job. Yet with all this he found time to preach, and went forth from time to time to bear the message of the Lord, and to warn the ungodly. Perhaps he preached to the audience that would watch him labour at the ark. In later days, in the time of Nehemiah, they held the sword in one hand and laboured with the trowel in the other.

Even when the flood was upon the earth his task still was not finished. During the period in the ark he had the daily care and feeding of all the animals, besides cleaning out their quarters. This was a constant seven-days-a week labour, but he was able for the commitment. Perhaps the sons helped him, the wives too, although Scripture is silent on this. Here is a lesson for believers, for there are many Martha's among the saints today, and they are not appreciated as they should be, but it is good to get on with the job as Noah did, and not grumble about it.

Noah saw the work through to its end. When the animals finally came forth from the ark they no doubt were healthy and well favoured, ready to start a new life. It is very easy to start a work; it is another thing to finish it. The Lord always finished His work; for example, He not only washed the disciples' feet, but He dried them as well with the towel; He did not leave them to finish the task. Again, when He raised the widow's son to life, He delivered him to his mother, thus completing the happiness to both mother and son. The principle is found first in Genesis 2 where several times the words are found, "Thus the heavens and the earth were finished, and all the host of them. And on the seventh day God ended his work which he had made; and he rested on the seventh day from all his work which he had made". So the principle lies at the very threshold of the Bible, and continues throughout its precious pages. How reassuring it is that in the work of salvation the Lord is the same, and has finished the blessing: "whom he called, them he justified; and whom he justified, them he also glorified". Presently we have the earnest, the first payment, in the gift of the Holy Spirit, proof that the complete salvation shall be enjoyed by all that believe.

That energy is also seen in the building of the altar. Now that no doubt was not a large construction and did not involve so much labour, but yet he did it. The simple lesson is that whether the task be small or great, he was a willing worker. Some want to do only the great things and have little time for the least, but the Lord taught that faithfulness in the least is as necessary as in the great. In passing it is worthy of note that the altar, although much smaller than the ark, accomplished a good deal more. The ark saved Noah and his family, the altar saved the world from future judgments with water.

Later he planted a vineyard. Now this required quite a lot of labour. It must be remembered that he was old at that time, and digging virgin soil entailed much labour, yet he was willing and able for this another task. To all the labour there must be added the constant caring and pruning that would be necessary in a vineyard. Finally the harvest and the vintage was heavy work; nothing was easy in horticulture in those days. A dozen men of the spiritual stature of Noah in our land today would "turn the world upside down" as in the days of the apostles. May the Lord raise up such that many of the tasks that cry out to be done will be accomplished before the Lord returns.

It is good to notice that the Lord was pleased with

NOAH

him and his work. He was made the means of blessing to others, so that the Lord did not bless apart from him: "Come thou and thy house into the ark" (7:1). Noah is named and singled out. Again, "Noah only remained alive, and those *with him* in the ark" (7:23). The same is seen at the beginning of chapter 6, "Noah found grace" (v.8); "God said to Noah" (v.13); "Make *thee* an ark" (v.14); "With *thee* will I establish my covenant" (v.18). So all blessing and safety was found in being with him; all centred on Noah. He is a picture of our Lord in this; the blessing of salvation and all that a man desires spiritually are found in association with Christ, and in Him alone. "In Him" is the usual formula in Ephesians. God will move only through Him, and we can approach only through Him; He is the one mediator between God and men.

Moreover he was a *godly* man. This of course was essential before the Lord could bless him, and make him the blessing that he was as the story unfolds. The Lord will cause the godly to approach unto Him. The godly man of Psalm 1 is like the tree planted by the rivers of water, bringing forth fruit in his season, his leaf will not wither, and whatsoever he does shall prosper. All this could be said of Noah. It is a profitable exercise to trace the traits of godliness in this man. Consider the beautiful words that describe him, "Noah found grace in the eyes of the Lord" (6:8,9). The eyes are symbolic of the Lord viewing his life; the Lord was scrutinising him, beholding him, and He saw the beauty of holiness there. "The eyes of the Lord are over the righteous and his ears are open unto his prayers" (Ps 34:15) would well apply here. The word "over" reads "upon, or towards", in the RV; the sweetness of the life that is godly is noticed by the Lord.

No doubt the grace mentioned in the verse refers to the Lord approaching in sovereign choice, but the fact

THE GODLY MAN

also remains as suggested earlier that Noah was not contaminated with the evil poison of the sons of God. Further statements are made in verse 9, and would that they were true of every child of God.

There are three marks of godliness in the verse. Noah was a just man. The RV terms him a righteous man, likely in his dealings with his fellow men. This is most remarkable when we consider the corruption that marked that generation. Were dealings in business underhand? Were corruption and bribery the order of the day? In the midst of this was found a man that was different. In business and in all his dealings he could be trusted; his honesty must have been rare in those dark days.

Not only was his life exemplary manward, it was also effective selfward: he was perfect in his generations, without blemish is the meaning of the word. Individually in his personal life and habits all was without blemish. The greater part of the life of any man is unseen by his fellow man, and the evils done in secret God will judge. Noah was somewhat different in this. The inward life was also approved by the Lord as was the outward life of the man.

But no doubt there is something deeper in the statement "without blemish, (or pure) in his generation". There had been none of that mixing with the blood from the terrible confusion that was characteristic of the times. He was fully human and without the awful mixture with the sons of God, the fallen angels as suggested in the previous pages.

The third statement is most beautiful, "He walked with God". Enoch was the first on record that walked with God, and God was so pleased with him that He took him to Himself, and the man never had the experience of dying. God would have others to follow in Enoch's footsteps. Here is another; he was not the first but

NOAH

nevertheless he is one of the few that are recorded in the Bible as having walked with God. To walk with God one must agree with Him, "Can two walk together except they be agreed" (Amos 3:3). Triads often occur in Scripture. A good example is found in Titus 2:12. "We should live soberly", that is towards the world, "righteously", as to one's personal sanctification, "and godly", that is Godward. The same construction is found again in 2 Peter 3:14, "That ye may be found of him in peace", that is towards fellow believers, "without spot", personally, as Jude, hating even the garment spotted by the flesh, and "blameless", that is before the world and the Lord. The Scriptures abound with these triple exhortations, but here in Genesis 6 we have the first occurrence.

This godliness is also seen in the repeated references to his obedience. This is more important in spiritual growth than people realise: "Behold to obey is better than sacrifice, and to hearken than the fat of rams" (1 Sam 15:22), so said Samuel to a very disobedient king Saul. The words of the Lord are so clear in this: "If you love me, keep my commandments" (John 14:15). This subject has previously been dealt with as one of the many features of Noah, but enlargement upon it is necessary as it is one of the great traits of this man. Therein lies the secret of God taking him up and making him a blessing to others. He walked with God, he was obedient to God: righteous in his life, he could well be a preacher of righteousness. Note his walk preceded his talk. God was not without a witness in those dark days: Enoch walked with God, and prophesied of the Lord's return; Noah walked with God, and preached righteousness to the people. How interesting it is that both men who witnessed in their time also walked with God. So it is required in every true child of God that

THE GODLY MAN

would seek to make Christ known; his calling is not only to preach, but also to walk in obedience to the Lord.

The third outstanding feature of this man is that he functioned as a *priest*, he built an altar, and he offered. This completes the full experience of the child of the Lord: his work at the ark and at preaching; his walk, as he had that close intimacy with the Lord, and finally his worship as a priest. Now the believer's life is comprised of these three elements. We work, or serve as bond slaves, serving not out of fear but out of love and devotion. We walk in testimony; this is essential to that work, so that on the one hand the blessing of the Lord will be forthcoming, and on the other, the people will listen. Then we worship. While we put this last it is the most important of all: "Thou shalt worship the Lord thy God, and him only shalt thou serve". So let us now examine priestly exercises as seen in Noah.

A priest draws near to God and has communion with Him. A further characteristic evident in Abraham as a priest is that he intercedes for others. The Aaronic priesthood especially was intended to function in this way, a picture of our Lord's intercession for others. In view of this, note the communion in the passages on Noah. In chapter 6:13 God said unto Noah, "The end of all flesh is come before me". This is real communion, for a friend will tell his heart to a friend. The Lord called the disciples friends because He informed them of what He was about to do. The same applies here, God let this man into His secret counsels. Again, in chapter 7:1 "The Lord said unto Noah, come thou, and all thy house into the ark; for thee have I seen righteous before me". See how God is revealing Himself, and speaking to the man; this is communion. But note, a righteous life is essential: God is holy, and without sanctification no man can see the Lord (Heb 12:14). To see implies to commune with

145

NOAH

Him, to come into His presence. Again, in chapter 8:15 God spake unto Noah, this time bidding him to come forth from the ark. So God was directing the movements of this man. Finally chapter 9:1 reads, "And God blessed Noah and his sons, and said unto them, Be fruitful, and multiply and replenish the earth". So it is evident the man held communion with the Lord. We can trace the blessedness of such exercise in the details that are given. It is good to learn in the presence of the Lord (6:3) as Mary did who sat at the feet of her Lord, and heard His Word. The same path is open to every believer to increase in the knowledge of the Lord. How fitting is the next communication (7:1), the leading of the Lord to place of safety, in this case into the ark. Chapter 8:16 has to do with God's time, He eventually makes known His will: now was the time to leave the ark. Noah did so, knowing fully that he was so directed by the Lord. Finally there was a communication of blessing in chapter 9:1, "be fruitful and multiply". There is great profit in being often in the presence of the Lord, and this is a very important part of priestly function.

But the altar in chapter 9 is the climax of this. Altars are most interesting in the Bible, and it would be a good thing first to consider the teaching behind the altars that men of God erected. The altar marks a place of sacrifice; later it was asociated with the burning of incense as in the tabernacle. Altars were often erected to commemorate an experience, so sometimes they were called memorials, such as that erected by the two and a half tribes on the east side of Jordan (Josh 22). They placed it by Jordan, not for sacrifice, but rather as a witness, a memorial that they had done their part, that they had helped in the war, and the Lord had granted them their inheritance on the other side of Jordan. In one sense Noah's altar was a memorial of the Lord preserving him through the flood.

THE GODLY MAN

Experience can really be seen in a great way in the four altars of Abraham. Therefore, an altar sums up a man's spiritual experience, and capacity because of the experience. But in those early days an altar must also be based upon the revelation of the Lord and the conveying of His mind, such as in the story of Abraham. This is the case here with Noah. Perhaps Abel had no altar, none is mentioned at any rate, because there is no recorded appearing of the Lord to him. Noah had great communications as already traced, so it is no wonder that the first altar appears in the Scriptures in his connection. An altar therefore indicates the character of God revealed, and His blessing in some way towards the person in question. Man appreciates, erects the altar, and shows thanksgiving and worship. Worship comes from the revelation of God; as He makes His ways known to man, man marvels and worships. Genesis 24:26 is a good example of this: the servant bowed down his head and worshipped the Lord when the Lord had revealed Himself as one that can direct aright. The main point of the altar then is, that God reveals Himself, the man appreciates the blessing that comes from that revelation, and worships. Faith has laid hold upon the Lord, the altar being the symbol of his worship. Abraham became the man of the altar; and what Noah started, Abraham made great. Of course the priest comes into all this, for later they were appointed to serve at the altar. Noah then is likely the first priest in the Bible.

His offerings are also most instructive. First, the building of the altar was spontaneous, there was no command from the Lord to erect it. He knew it would be pleasing to the Lord, so he built the altar, and it was so timely. The same can be said of his offerings. No direction came from the Lord, yet he knew exactly what to offer and could distinguish the clean from the unclean. This shows the spiritual intelligence of the man. Later Israel had instruction as to what was unclean and what was not (Lev 11), but this man needed no such thing. He was able to discern the mind of the Lord, and in his actions he brought pleasure to the Lord. In Malachi chapter 1 the people of Israel were offering that which was not acceptable to the Lord, that which was unclean with blemishes, in spite of the instruction of Leviticus chapter 11. How different was Noah, who needed no such teaching because his mind was in tune with the Lord's and he knew that the best was for the Lord, and according to the Lord's requirements. Ask him the question, "Why the clean animals?" and he would answer, "The Lord is holy". He had witnessed it in the judgment of the flood, he knew, and admired, perhaps feared the holiness of the Lord. Again, ask him, "Why so many offerings?" he would answer, "The Lord is good". He had manifested His great mercy, and was worthy of the best. Note also that they are burnt offerings. Now in the early books of the Bible the burnt offering also served as a sin offering, the distinction was not made until the Levitical offerings were written from the mouth of the Lord by the hand of Moses. While that is so, there is no doubt that Noah meant these as a thank offering, a deep appreciation; all was for God. He is worthy of all we have and are. Now many offerings went up from men, but were they accepted? Think of the insincere offering of Malachi chapter 1, and that of Cain in Genesis chapter 4. But here the heart was sincere; Noah was so genuine. Perhaps this was the first real burnt offering, being all for God. He was giving of the best, and there was so much; it was all for God. The priestly man Noah is a great pattern for us all.

The man of like passions as ourselves shall be considered in the next chapter.

20

THE TWO NATURES

Human nature cannot be improved. This comes out in Noah. True, he was a priest, he was an obedient man and an energetic servant, but he was also a man of like passion as we ourselves. He started well and continued well, but did not end so well.

The birds are most important, and the Lord has not set them in the passage just for colour, but rather for moral lessons. First, he sent forth a raven, an unclean bird according to Leviticus 11:13-15, "And every raven after its kind". We become aware of this when in experience we first taste of the old nature received through the fall of Adam. All are born at a distance from God and facing in the wrong direction; we are as Cain who went out from the presence of the Lord. The raven went to and fro until the waters were dried up from the earth. The world had just undergone a terrible judgment, but the raven was content with that state of affairs. Even so the old nature is happy with a world under the judgment of God. The world is found guilty; it is only a matter of time until the sentence passed is carried out. The man of the world is content with this, in fact he knows nothing else. The raven must have fed on the carcasses of the dead as they drifted on the surface of the waters. It is sad if believers, in spite of being saved from the coming judgment, are entangled with the world and the desires of the old nature.

149

NOAH

The dove however is different, setting forth the new nature of the believer. Again the principle appears: first the natural, then that which is spiritual. The words describing the sending forth of the dove are interesting. He "sent forth" the raven, but "he sent forth a dove *from him*". This is beautiful, suggesting that the new nature comes from the Lord Himself, given that being a saviour Noah resembles the Lord. So the new nature comes from the Lord; the new life is received when the Spirit enters and we are born from above. Consequently, the dove found no rest for the sole of her feet, she could not be content. Being a clean bird she could neither feed nor rest on that which is dead. The raven may, but not the dove. The wording "the sole of her foot" is important, as being linked with the reference in Joshua chapter 1: the people of God were to possess only that on which the sole of their foot rested. Much land there was to be possessed, but the resting of the sole of the foot on it was a claim to that land. We rest on the blessings of God in Christ, but we can learn these wonderful things, and rest upon them, and enjoy them. If we do we shall not rest upon that which is condemned and savours of death. The dove then, finding no rest for the sole of her feet returned to him, back to the shelter of the ark. Our continual coming to the Lord, our communion, our strength, our shelter are all in Him. Noah put forth his hand and took her, and drew her to him into the ark. The teaching is lovely here. Sometimes we wander a little, the eye of our God, of whom Noah is a picture, is upon us. We return, His hand is upon us, He pulls, attracts us, draws us to Himself, and into the safety of the ark. Restoration is here; it is the experience of the child of God very often.

The dove was sent forth from the ark a second time; the new world was forming, growth was there, and the dove returned with the olive leaf in her mouth. The olive tree in Romans chapter 11 is the symbol of the favour of God. Saints of this age are the wild branches grafted in, the Gentiles have been favoured by the Lord in a wonderful way in this time of grace. Here was the earnest of new life, that of the Spirit. The dove plucked it off (Gen. 8:11), meaning that growth was there, a bush, a tree, so much more than she had brought. We enjoy things that are divine through the divine nature that we possess, but it is only a plucking from the abundance that exists, the land must be possessed. These two thoughts go together therefore, the sole of the foot, and the plucked leaf. Both speak of the abundance that is available for our new natures to feed upon. To be carnally minded is death, such is the raven, but to be spiritually minded is life and peace. This is the dove, the mind that feeds upon the things of the Spirit. The question is, what do we feed upon? The old saints used to express it so well in saying, "Whatever nature we feed the most, will come out on top".

The third time the dove was sent forth from the ark it returned not again. The new world, the new creation had been entered into. Noah himself went forth from the ark, but the dove went before him. The experience of the new creation had altogether captivated the bird. All this was a lesson to Noah, for he had understanding of the clean and unclean birds and what was acceptable to the Lord. Yet the thing in which he was so well versed, was the very thing in which he fell down. So often people fail in their strong point. Such was seemingly the case with Noah; his lapse in the latter part of chapter 9 is sad reading. He began to be a husbandman, he planted a vineyard, and was the first it would seem to produce the blood of the grape, the intoxicating wine. Whether knowingly or ignorantly he went to excess, and soon became drunken. His drunkenness was such that he was in a stupor, a drunken sleep. He was not watching now as in the past, and he was naked within the tent. Here is a remarkable parallel with Adam and the fall.

Both went into error concerning a tree, the tree of the knowledge of good and evil in the case of Adam, and in Noah's case the vine. Does one not learn from the failure of others? Noah it seems did not.

Again, they were both naked; as was Adam so was Noah, he was naked within the tent. It was a return to the fall, the source of the nature that is devoid of the Lord, which came upon all mankind (Rom 5:12). He went back to the state of the first man, as he disobeyed the word of the Lord.

The curse followed in both cases. Adam brought the curse on all his posterity, and Noah brought the curse upon the seed of Canaan, the son of Ham. Instead of removing the curse as Lamech thought, it was rather increased, and especially to the sons of Canaan.

It is sad to see him drunken. There is no activity now, the giant in obedience and blessing is now helpless upon the ground. There is no preaching now, no building as in the past. Also the lovely discernment has failed him, he cannot discern the terrible consequences of strong drink. Alas many millions have been snared by the same thing throughout the ages. It all resulted from the abundance of the new world, the place of prosperity. Here was a covenant, the blessing of the Lord, food, increase and all that man needed in an abundance he had never known before. This led to his downfall, as in the case of so many. Paul warns the rich, "they that will be rich" (1 Tim 6:9). It was their own will not the Lord's self will. Some believers grasp after riches whom the Lord never intended to be rich, and the desired riches become a snare. Others He prospers. This is the Lord's

THE TWO NATURES

doing, and such have a great stewardship to use the God given riches to His glory. To one He gives knowledge, to another leadership, to another the ability to preach, and, we could say, to another riches. All are responsible for the things that God has rendered into their hands. "What hast thou that thou didst not receive?" (1 Cor 4:7). So Noah was put to sleep by the prosperity of the new world.

Individuals can fail in this respect, but so also can churches as in the case of Loadica. Prosperity was their downfall. They said, "I am rich, and increased with goods, and have need of nothing", yet they knew not they were wretched, miserable, poor, blind and naked. All this could well describe Noah; he did not make rich as the apostle, "as poor, yet making many rich" (2 Cor 6:10). Noah made some poor, very poor indeed as the curse took effect. Surely after the whole episode he must have felt most miserable.

So ends the outline of this great man, for this is what he was in spite of the failure at the close: an energetic man, one above many, an obedient man, the joy and the delight of the Lord. He was too a priestly man, who could approach the Lord in intelligence, and bring delight to the very heart of the Lord, but also just a man, who could fail just as so many believers fail. In a sense this is a consolation.

Most believers certainly could be more energetic in the things of the Lord, saints could be more obedient, and His commandments are not grievous, and we could be more priestly. The great truth of the priesthood of all believers is a priceless treasure. In all this we can follow him. But we have no need to follow him in his failure, in his drunken sleep. Paul warns, "They that sleep sleep in the night; and they that be drunken are drunken in the night" (1 Thess 5:7), this should not be the character of

NOAH

the sons of light, we belong to a position greater even than Noah; we have the Spirit within, the Spirit that *used* Noah *dwells* in us now.

21

THE LORD MANIFESTED IN GENESIS 6

Now we approach the history of the Genesis flood, and we shall follow the example of Peter. That is, we shall try to glean from the workings of the Lord something of His ways, and attributes. In everything that happens in our lives, the hand of the Lord can be seen, so, from the least to the greatest in the history of the world of men, the Lord is wonderfully manifested. It has often been said that the Lord writes history as well as giving prophecy. Prophecy is really history written in advance: all history had been in the mind of God before the events actually took place. So we turn to the history of the flood again, taking the lead from Peter in his epistles, to trace the ways of the Lord. This we shall do first from chapter 6.

The first reference is in verse 3. "And the Lord said, My Spirit shall not always strive with man, for that he also is flesh: yet his days shall be an hundred and twenty years." This is a very difficult verse, often used in the gospel but somewhat out of context. The passage is generally used to teach that the spirit here is the Holy Spirit of God, and that He convicts of sin, but that He can stop striving with the soul if no response is forthcoming. Other passages definitely teach this, the history of Judas for example, but it is doubtful whether this is the meaning here. Yet the verse has been used mightily of the Lord in the conversion of souls. God can use a passage like this, and similar verses such as Revelation 3:20, although they are preached out of context.

Some difficulties appear in the gospel interpretation. The word "strive" can be translated "abide ... forever", as some versions put it, (e.g. RV margin). Again, what is meant by "for that he also is flesh"? what has this to do with sinners being convicted and saved? Also, why one hundred and twenty years? a much longer time than the Spirit speaks to sinners today. So difficulties remain that must be faced. It helps to interpret the verse if the reason for the flood is kept in mind: the mingling of the sons of God with the women descended from the man Adam; this is the context.

My spirit surely is the life, the breath of life that was given to man in the first place: "God ... breathed into his nostrils the breath of life; and man became a living soul". The God who gave this life was going to take it away again. All living should die at once, by the flood, and the time between the prophecy and its fulfilment would be one hundred and twenty years. Twenty years after this statement the call of Noah took place; one hundred years later the flood came and the abiding spirits in the bodies of the then generation were taken away, and are now in prison (1 Pet 3). Therefore the time was set by the Lord; one hundred and twenty years would pass and then the judgment would descend.

Again, what is meant by "he also is flesh". There have often been attempts by man to be equal with God. The devil puts such thoughts into the heart, as he did to the first woman, "ye shall be as gods" (Gen 3:5). The eating of the tree of knowledge of good and evil was an attempt to be equal with God. The same could be said of the tower of Babel in chapter 11 which was to reach up to heaven. The same applies here also to the sons of God, if we are right in interpreting that they are angels. The

THE LORD MANIFESTED IN GENESIS 6

women were willing to be joined to them so as to produce children that were different, supernatural. They were striving after something that was not in the purpose of God for man. It could be written over the whole affair, "We shall be like God". God reminds man that he is still flesh, the same flesh, and this flesh cannot be altered even though it mingle with angels. So the passage is saying that man is still the same fallen man of flesh, angel seed or no. God said, "I will put an end to all this seed" meaning by the flood in one hundred and twenty years time. Then, "I will take my spirit, the life", and indeed death came to all except those in the safety of the ark. Noah was spared, and his family; they were not polluted with the unlawful union with angels. The preaching of Noah did not start until he was at least five hundred years old, probably during the time he was building the ark; the flood came when he was six hundred years old. This period of one hundred years is short of the one hundred and twenty in verse 3, and is not a reference to the building time for the ark. Therefore this verse does not apply to the striving of the Holy Spirit with people during the preaching of Noah, or to the building of the ark. The Spirit was present in the testimony and preaching of Noah as 1 Peter 3 teaches, but this verse is not a reference to that. Suffice it to say that God enters and controls the affairs of men.

This likely was the beginning of the shortening of the life of man upon the earth. Until this time nine hundred years was the normal. After the flood the length of life lessened; Moses lived until he was an hundred and twenty, today few reach the hundred mark. This could be one of the many passages of Scripture that have a double significance. If so, the one hundred and twenty years are (1) the years until the flood should come, (2) the years of man's life expectancy.

NOAH

But we must proceed to the manifestation of God in the chapter. Here there is a presentation of the omniscience of God, He knows all, nothing is hidden from Him. "God saw that the wickedness of man was great in the earth, and that every imagination of the thoughts of his heart was only evil continually" (v. 5). Again, "God looked upon the earth, and, behold, it was corrupt; for all flesh had corrupted his way upon the earth" (v. 12). The Lord is aware of all the sinful deeds of every man, and also of the thoughts from which they spring. "God shall judge the secrets of men by Christ Jesus" (Rom 2:16). "Every idle word that men shall speak, they shall give account thereof in the day of judgment" (Matt 12:36). At the great white throne (Rev 20) the books will be opened, and the dead will be judged according to their works. God has a record of all that every person has done in the body. Not that God needs books; the language is symbolic of the infinite mind and wisdom of God. Psalm 50 puts this thought in a very searching way: He will set out the sins in the order in which they were committed before the eyes of the guilty. This is true not only of the unsaved, but of the saved also. Paul speaks of the things done in the body being judged at the judgment seat of Christ (2 Cor 5:10). God is aware of all the things done in the lifetime of the believer. So much of the past is forgotten by self and others, but all is known to the Lord. Again, God "will bring to light the hidden things of darkness, and will make manifest the counsels of the hearts: and then shall every man have praise of God" (1 Cor 4:5).

This is in a good sense of course; the Corinthians were critical of Paul, decrying his motives, but Paul looks forward to the judgment seat of Christ, when the motives of the heart will be made known. The same thought occurs in Philippians 4:3, "those...whose names are in the book of life" are labourers in the gospel and in work of the Lord.

In our passage all the corruption and all the wickedness is known to the Lord. The flood was God's answer to the persistent sins of mankind. The most searching factor here is that the Lord knows the "imagination", or thoughts of the heart. The heart is the real person; where the heart is there the treasure is also; we count as treasure what is valued in the heart. The words of our Lord are enlightening, "For from within, out of the heart of men, proceed evil thoughts, adulteries, fornication, murders" (Mark 7:21). Note the parallels between this verse and Genesis 6: *the thoughts*, "out of the heart", "every imagination of the thoughts of his heart was only evil continually"; *the corruption,* "adulteries, fornication", "all flesh had corrupted his way"; the violence, "murders", "the earth was filled with violence". One could say that Mark 7:21 is a commentary on the people of Genesis 6.

The Lord who sees the evil, knows the motive of all, knows the depravity, and knows the rebellion must judge all this in keeping with His holy Nature: "The end of all flesh is come before me; for the earth is filled with violence... I will destroy them with the earth" (v. 13). The sad thing with many believers, and especially those that take a lead in the churches, is that they are aware of the sins of some, but do nothing about it in the way of discipline. Such was the case at Corinth: a man had committed a grievous sin, but he still was allowed to take his place among the believers (1 Cor 5). The same applies to the churches of Revelation chapters 2 and 3. Sins were apparent, evil doctrine was held and taught, but the leaders seemingly were powerless to do anything in the way of judgment. To carry out discipline one needs righteousness, wisdom, authority and love; the

NOAH

Lord has all four. Wisdom is needed to discern the real guilt of the people, righteousness to judge accordingly, and the authority to be able to carry it through. Over all is love: it is for the good of the company and the person in question. The Lord here sees the evil, in righteousness He shows His disapproval, and with great authority and power overthrows the world with the engulfing flood. Noah and his family see the grace of God, His love fully manifested in their salvation. The very nature and ways of God are paramount in this great passage. The government of God is prominent in Scripture. Examples abound such as the judgment of Egypt, and Israel in the wilderness and in the land. Daniel speaks much of this government in his book of visions and prophecies about the nations, past and future. His chief theme is the times of the Gentiles, God using the nations to punish Israel for their idolatry, and then in turn punishing those nations for going beyond what He had intended in the punishment of Israel. The church in the New Testament is not exempt from government either. Peter again, speaks of judgment beginning at the house of God (1 Pet 4:17). The Acts records the judgment upon Ananias and Sapphira, who lied against the Holy Spirit and suffered the penalty of death.

Another point to be noted is that the judgment does not fall immediately. The Lord is longsuffering, He always leaves space for repentance as in the church at Thyatira. (Rev 2:21). God allows the sin to develop, and leaves room for the people to turn from their sin and unto the Lord. Such is the case here. The 120 years before the judgment fell was a measure of the longsuffering of God, as Peter reminds us (1 Pet 3:20). God is neither hurried nor hindered in His plans. He is not in a hurry to judge sin, but will eventually judge in righteousness. This principle is seen in the New Testament: the father did not seek to stop the prodigal in his resolve to leave home, he let the son go his way, he let the sin develop. Had the boy not repented, the judgment of the Lord would have consumed him; he was near the end when he had the will to turn. Again, in the parable of the wheat and tares, the Master would allow both to grow together until the harvest, then there will be the separation of the tares from the wheat for burning. Another passage teaching this principle is Revelation 14:18-19. The angel is told, "Thrust in thy sharp sickle and gather the clusters of the vine of the earth; for her grapes are fully ripe". The Lord then lets sin develop, leaves space for repentance, then if there is no response, He righteously judges.

Thus it is evident that the Lord is seen as omniscient, patient, longsuffering, and faithful to His promise of judgment.

22

SALVATION IS OF THE LORD

Another great characteristic of the Lord seen here is that He favours people, His sovereign grace reached out to Noah. As we have sought to explain earlier, Noah was not corrupted, and this was acceptable to the Lord, yet grace cannot be ruled out. "He will have mercy on whom he will have mercy" (Rom 9:15). Noah found grace; the grace was not in himself; it was not merit; the grace came from the Lord. The result of this salvation was that he walked with God, and was different, as we have traced, from others in his generation. He was upright in the midst of a corrupt society. The sons also came in for the blessing, again by the grace of God. Peter reminds us that eight souls were saved by water; "saved", all was of the Lord. But it would be to our profit to see that there are certain things that are very acceptable to the Lord, such as the righteous life that was displayed in Noah, and his purity from blemish personally. He was clean from the terrible habits of the then world without God.

As for his walk with God, God wants the fellowship and company of those whom He has redeemed. He desires the saved person to talk with Him and to walk with Him. This longing on the part of God is still the same. The Lord will cause the godly to come near to Himself. Nevertheless this walking with God is wonderful grace, condescending grace indeed that we are permitted to walk with Him at all, that we can please Him. All is in

SALVATION IS OF THE LORD

Christ, for He has brought us to this near position. It is more marvellous still that He moderates His step so that we can keep pace with Him. How else should a child walk with a full grown man? the strides are so different in length. How great is our position in Christ that it can be so. The Lord tenderly brings us along, carries us betimes, and waits for us to understand.

Noah was hardly looking for reward in this walk, it was reward enough to be able to do so. Enoch was the first man in the Bible of whom it is said that "he walked with God". It must have been a very happy experience for Enoch, but something better lay before him: God took him to Himself without dying. Noah's walk with God was not with a view to being saved from the flood; in fact the walk is mentioned before he received any intimation that a flood was to come. His walk issued from a heart that loved the Lord. Paul was willing to lose all for the excellency of the knowledge of his Lord (Phil 3:8). Yet the walk of Noah resulted in his salvation from the flood judgment that came upon all. However faith was in the man, and God honoured that faith. Without faith it is impossible to please God (Heb 11:6). To walk with God is really to keep in step with His will. Note the five references to walk in Ephesians.

1. Walk worthily of the vocation wherewith you are called (4:1). This is positive.
2. Walk not as the Gentiles, a different walk (4:17). This would be negative.
3. Walk in love (5:2).
4. Walk in light (5:8).
5. Walk as wise, not as fools (5:15).

This entails the will of the Lord, in keeping with the vocation, the new life in Christ, and in contrast to the

NOAH

old. We must not walk as previously we did, as Gentiles without the knowledge of the Lord. It is walking in love, in contrast to the past hatred of divine things; walking in light, so different from the former sphere of darkness; and walking as wise, not foolish as the man without God. Noah was in step with the will of the God he had found, and consequently was different from those around him. Again, to walk with the Lord is to go in the same direction as He, in keeping with the outworking of His purpose.

These beautiful traits were delightfully manifested in the walk of Noah with the Lord.

The Lord is again seen as revealing His will. Detailed instruction was given to Noah regarding the dimensions of the ark and its materials; nothing was left to his own imagination. "Make thee an ark" (Gen 6:14) was the voice of divine authority, there was no plea of any sort from the Lord. A command from the Lord must be obeyed or else one suffers the consequences. It was a clear command, he knew exactly what he was to do, all the instructions were precise. God does not give any commands in a veiled way, but the Word is clear and distinct. If it seems otherwise it is because we have not the eyes to see. Again, the command was for the good of the man, it was in his interest, and for the glory of the Lord that commanded. All the instruction that the Lord gives to His people has these ends, and it would be to the profit of believers to hearken and obey.

The instructions given to Noah concerning the building of the ark are therefore worthy of consideration. Just as the tabernacle building had deep typical meaning, so also has the ark. The many details are not given to fill pages, God has principles therein.

First, the measurements, 300 cubits long, 50 cubits wide, and 30 cubits high, all are multiples of ten. Now ten is the number of responsibility in Scripture, as the ten commandments. The ten fingers on the hands of man mark his responsibility to work for God, and ten toes indicate his responsibility to walk with God. Noah fulfilled both of these, he walked with God, and he laboured with the hands in building the ark. This runs all through the New Testament. Once a man becomes a follower of Christ, he takes His yoke upon him, and becomes submissive to his Lord. This Noah did: he took the yoke of service upon his soul, following the principle of Matthew 11:20-30. His name means rest, and he certainly found rest for his soul. The first words of Saul of Tarsus after he was saved were, "Lord, what wilt thou have me to do", and this ought to be the cry of every new born soul. Even into eternity we shall serve Him: "his servants shall serve him" (Rev 22:3).

The material was gopher wood. Typically, wood speaks of humanity in the Scriptures, and as man we serve. Adam was a man with the responsibility to serve. The Lord became a servant automatically by becoming a man, He took upon Himself the form of a servant, being made in the likeness of men (Phil 2:7).

However, this was Noah on resurrection ground. The trees were cut down, then built into the ark. Such is the standing of every child of the Lord. He has died in Christ, but has been given life in Christ also, and in coming to Christ was built as a stone into the building (1 Pet 2). Gopher wood is not mentioned any where else in the Bible. Many suggest it is the cypress tree, or one like it that has a resin content. This agrees with the word "pitch" in verse 14, which seemingly comes from a Hebrew word meaning resin, and not bitumen. However, the type is sure; we are human, yet in newness of life, serving the Lord.

The word "pitch" is instructive. The Hebrew word

means to cover, and is translated "atone" throughout the Old Testament. Only by being covered by the work of the Saviour can a man have standing before the Lord and produce anything acceptable to Him in service. Faith comes in here, Noah had this faith (Heb 11:7). This was accounted to him for righteousness, as covered with the provision of God in Christ. Note, the ark was pitched within and without, within for the eye of God: "the Lord knoweth them that are his", but without also: "let him that nameth the name of Christ depart from iniquity" (2 Tim 2:19). "Thy sins be forgiven thee", the Lord said to the palsied man, that was the record in heaven for the eye of God. The Lord also commanded the man, "Rise, take up thy bed, and go unto thine house", and he rose up took his bed and walked before them all, that was the witness on the earth. A work within is necessary else there is no salvation, but the evidence without ought to be present also with every believer.

"Rooms shalt thou make in the ark". The word is nests, no doubt speaking of the different compartments in the ark, some for the animals and others for the humans. The Lord uses the idea of a nest as a resting place. "Birds of the air have nests, but the Son of man hath not where to lay his head" (Matt 8:20): the Lord had no resting place as far as earth was concerned. These rooms, or nests, speak of the rest all believers have in the Lord. The Lord speaks of this: "Come unto me all ye that labour...I will give you rest" (Matt 11:28).

The rooms also carry the thought of separation. Now Noah was truly separated in every way, but the truth is binding upon all the people of the Lord, as is enjoined in 2 Cor 6:14-18. The walk as seen in Eph 4, is to stand in contrast to that of the Gentiles that know not God. The same idea is found in 1 Thess 4:5, "not [living] in the lust of concupiscence, even as the Gentiles, that know not

SALVATION IS OF THE LORD

God". They had turned to God from idols; there was a complete separation from former companions and the past ways of life. This should touch every department of the life of the believer: private life, family life, business life, and of course assembly life. The coming of the Lord is so presented in 1 Thessalonians: it touches every facet of our lives: devotion in chapter one, service in chapter two, holy living in chapter three, family and loved ones in chapter four and so on. The "nest principle" takes us away from the pursuits of the world and the flesh, and contents itself in the secure rest in Christ.

The measurements used in the construction of the ark are perfectly balanced. The larger ships of today follow the same proportions to give them stabilityin the water. Balance is a great thing with which every saint should be endowed. James 1 speaks of that maturity that is reached by experience and by the Word. Both together are required to make the mature man. To have one without the other is to be off balance. A man of the Word only lacks experience; a man of experience only lacks the knowledge of what God has to say about the matter in question.

Balance is also required in giving, "not that other men be eased, and you burdened: But by an equality" (2 Cor 8:13). Again, in the matter of separation in 1 Cor 5:10 Paul delineates a balanced course. We are to be in the world but not of it; the same idea is found in John 17:14-15. Again, the Lord taught His disciples not to be like the Pharisees who taught the truth but did not practise it. Believers should teach and practise, to be ethical, doing as well as teaching. It is balance that the Lord requires from His people.

The next detail concerns the window. God is practical: man must have fresh air, ventilation is needed. Also he must be able to see out. The window it seems went all

167

the way around the ark. It was not a little window in the roof as some imagine. The RV reads, "light shalt thou make to the ark and to a cubit shalt thou finish it upward" (Gen 6:16); natural light could enter the ark. It would seem that there was a continual window at the least to one of the three stories; this space was a cubit in depth. Whatever the exact arrangement was may not be determined, but surely some spiritual lessons can be inferred.

Noah must see out, and from this window he eventually sent forth the birds. A believer should be aware of what is happening around him. This point is often brought up in Scripture. "Beloved, be not ignorant of this one thing" (2 Pet 3:8): we should be aware of what the Lord is doing among the nations, and of the times. "Not forsaking the assembling of ourselves together" (Heb 10:25). The writer was aware that some saints had stopped going to the meetings, and it was a matter of concern to him. From the report of Chloe, it is evident that Chloe was aware of the state of the Corinthian church, was concerned about it, and reported it to Paul. This was not gossip, rather it was a cry for help. The Corinthians themselves were not aware that things had slipped, but others like Chloe had the "window".

Epaphroditus of Philippi was able to inform Paul of the things concerning the church there, both good and bad; he also had a "window". The Lord was aware of the tower that fell on the people of Siloam, of the number that were killed, and also of the blood that Pilate had mingled with the sacrifices of the people. The Lord of course was observant. He knew the events of the times and the thoughts of the people concerning these things. Paul speaks of the difficulty of the times at that period in Corinth, and advises not to marry. The burdens that marriage brings would only add to the hardships they

SALVATION IS OF THE LORD

were passing through at the time (1 Cor 7:26).

It is good to be conversant with the times and not to be too self centred, to have the eyes open to the need, as the Lord exhorted in John 4, "Lift up your eyes, and look on the fields; for they are white already to harvest". It is wise to see the writing on the wall for this old world soon to undergo judgment. This, coupled with the drift of saints and the general decline in spiritual things, needs to be observed. All should be using the window of survey and interest in what is happening around us. As it turned out, the birds especially had to do with this window and, as was considered, these are typical of the two natures in every believer. The window is a necessity in the life of the believer in order to know himself. Paul said, "For I know that in me (that is in my flesh,) dwelleth no good thing" (Rom 7:18). Again, "I know nothing against myself; yet am I not hereby justified" (1 Cor 4:4). A Christian needs to know that the old nature is still present with him and can be exceedingly troublesome at times. We ought to use the window on ourselves. In this respect 2 Cor 12 is very interesting: the beginning of the chapter reveals how far a believer can go in spiritual experiences. Paul speaks of one caught up into the third heaven, into paradise, who heard things unutterable on earth. However, the end of the chapter manifests how far the old nature, if uncontrolled, will bring down the believer; he speaks of those who have not repented of the uncleanness, fornication and the lasciviousness that they have committed. In conclusion of this matter, the believer ought to be cognizant of the happenings in the world, in the church, and in his own heart. In writing his second epistle, Peter first speaks of the condition of the true believer in chapter one, then of the condition of Christendom in chapter two, and finally of the prevailing unbelief in the world in chapter four, he was using the

NOAH

window.

This is followed by three narratives which speak of elevation and development. The Lord would have His people to be constantly developing upwards. Progress is stamped on all that the Lord does. This can be seen in the successive days in Genesis 1. Again, in the course of revelation God progressively revealed Himself: first in power in creation, then personally to men in communication and vision, and then in the holiness of His nature at Sinai. Israel experienced God in discipline and in His ways in the wilderness, they learned His thoughts and purposes in the prophets. The high noon of the revelation of God came in His beloved Son who made known the very heart of God. Yet all truth awaited the coming of the Spirit at Pentecost. The revelation is now complete: we have all the word of God. Such a pattern of progress could not be equalled.

Elizabeth in Luke 1 dwelt in the hill country, she had the wisdom of the Lord. The Lord's greatest revelation of His personal glory was upon a mountain top, namely, the transfiguration. Mark's account of the parable of the sower highlights the development in fruitfulness: thirtyfold, sixtyfold, and one hundredfold (Mark 4:8). When Matthew relates the same parable he reverses this order (Matt 13), beginning with one hundredfold and ending with thirty. The reason for this seems to be that the King is reviewing the servants rather than the fruitfulness of the seed. The same pattern is seen in the parable of the talents: the Lord begins with the man who had five and ends with him who had only one. Matthew is dealing with the King, but Mark with development. A parable unique to the Gospel of Mark is found in chapter 4, that of the growth of the seed; note the developing order; "first the blade, then the ear, after that the full corn in the ear" (v. 28). The Lord used strong language in upbraiding the disciples in the boat because of their weak understanding of His ministry (Mark 8); their lack of development was grievous to the Lord. They did not understand what He meant by the leaven of the Pharisees and of Herod.

Such is chapter 6 of Genesis: a manifestation of the greatness of God in salvation and in provision for His own. The Lord is seen in other ways, but these will be dealt with in another chapter.

23

FAITHFULNESS AND FOOD

The Lord is manifested in many of His ways in Genesis 6. Some of these have already been considered, but an outstanding characteristic of the Lord is His faithfulness. He is a covenant keeping God in verse 18, He will be faithful to His promises. We are saved, not on the ground of human merit, but on the basis of the work of the Lord Jesus alone, and God will be faithful to our simple acceptance of this. Verse 18 was yet future: "With thee will I establish my covenant"; it was fully accomplished in chapter 9. God's purpose for the saint is to eventually glorify him, and nothing can hinder this from being so: "whom he justified, them he also glorified" (Rom 8:30). All is well, we have a faithful God.

Alongside of this we see the power of God, for faithfulness has no hope without power. He was able to bring in the flood to destroy, "Behold, I even I, do bring a flood of waters upon the earth, to destroy all flesh" (v. 17). The Lord also had the power to deliver, as Noah and family experienced. The flood was not an accident or a freak of nature but was a deliberate act of the power of God. It was noted in an earlier chapter that the Lord just reversed what had taken place in the process of Genesis 1: the earth overflowed with water and perished (see 2 Pet 3). The Lord needed no help to accomplish this. He is the sovereign Lord of all creation. All must obey Him, even the elements. As the Lord is complete in creation, so also is He in judgment as Romans chapter 2 makes clear: none shall escape. John saw "the dead, small and great, stand before God" (Rev 20:12). The fact that they were small or of no great significance on earth will not hide them in the day of wrath. Greatness will not be a saving merit, nor smallness a saviour; all shall perish that lived without the Saviour, Christ Jesus the Lord. For the Christian too, judgment must begin at the house of God. Paul reminds the saints that "every one of us shall give account of himself to God" (Rom 14:12).

We see also the importance to God of life. To preserve life Noah was instructed not only to enter the ark himself, but to bring in the animals as well, that living things would enter the new world. To this end too the command was given to store food, after all the creatures must eat during the season in the ark. It is interesting that God is always putting emphasis on food. Trees for food were paramount in the garden of Eden, and Genesis ends with a famine. Yet there was food in Egypt, thanks to Joseph, and so the descendants of Jacob remained alive. Note the references to food in this chapter.

1. It was necessary; no life can be sustained without it. For the believer, spiritual food is required if the new life is to be sustained. Hence, Peter speaks of desiring the sincere milk of the Word (1 Pet 2), and Paul speaks of feeding with milk, then with the meat (1 Cor 3).
2. "Take unto thee of all food that is eaten" (v. 21). Variety is taken note of by God: a balanced diet is necessary for healthy living. The same principle holds good in the spiritual realm. There is devotional ministry that we might love our Lord, ethical ministry that we might be practical Christians, doctrine that we may appreciate the grand position into which the Lord has brought us, and prophecy that we might not be

NOAH

ignorant of what God is doing and will yet do in this world. All these lines of ministry, and others beside, are necessary for the sustaining of the life received from the Lord.

Paul in writing to the Corinthians sums up ministry in three words: edification, exhortation and comfort (1 Cor 14:3). He himself is the example of this in 2 Thessalonians. The first chapter is a passage that provides great comfort, "rest with us, when the Lord Jesus shall be revealed" (v. 7). The second chapter is one of edification. The apostle sets at rest their troubled minds by the doctrine of the Lord's return (vv. 1-2). Finally the third chapter deals with exhortation. Three times he commands them, and he uses the word "exhort" in verse 12.

Again, these three lines of ministry are suggested in 1 Cor 3 by the metaphors of gold, silver, and precious stones, in contrast to wood, hay, stubble. The first three would symbolize profitable ministry, the latter three that which was of little worth. Paul uses a little irony there, as they were building into the assembly the wisdom of the world instead of the wisdom taught by the Spirit of which he had spoken in chapter 2. The wisdom they were using was easily found as are wood, hay and stubble; the gathering of them involved little energy in comparison with the deep searching and laborious mining for the precious minerals.

3. All this had to be gathered by Noah and involved much labour. Of course he laboured with the future in mind to feed all that would be in the ark. "Thou shalt gather it to thee" (v. 21). So it is with the minister of the Word; he must be continually gathering and have a good store in readiness for the days to come.
4. Noah had first to consider himself in all this provision:

FAITHFULNESS AND FOOD

"food for thee and for them" (v.21); the teacher must first feed himself. He also must be sustained; he is in need of growth as well as those to whom he ministers, and is in danger from the world, the flesh, and the devil as others. The lessons are as necessary for him as for the sheep he seeks to feed.

5. The order is very important in verse 21: "for thee, and for them", first for self and then for others. This is the opposite of service in which others are to be considered rather than self. Of this principle the Lord is the great example (Phil 2). Ministry must be applied first to oneself, then it will prove to be a blessing to others. A New Testament passage bears this out: "Take heed unto thyself, and unto the doctrine; continue in them: for in doing this thou shalt both save thyself, and them that hear thee" (1 Tim 4:16).

6. As for the flock, the minister must make sure they are being fed. He must really feel his responsibility to feed, and not to be slack either in the gathering or in the distribution of his material. It is human to continue ministering without the freshness from the Lord that is required. Again, one must have the confidence of the saints to speak and teach; the gift must be recognized and the life must be in keeping.

This is no doubt what is meant by "continue in them"; the teacher is to make the teaching part of his life and character so the confidence of the saints will be stimulated when they listen. Again, the food must be attractively presented: teaching must be orderly. After all, God is not the author of confusion but of order.

If these few principles were adhered to, the ministry would prove to be wholesome for the people of God, all would learn and spiritual growth would be enhanced.

In considering this reference to food the teacher has

175

been the centre of focus, but surely the evangelist is there as well. The real purpose of the ark was to preserve life, to keep alive. Souls were saved because of Noah, after all he was a preacher of righteousness. The response came not from the people but from his own family. In type, he was one of the first evangelists in the Bible. Again, he is seen as a pastor, or shepherd; he had the care of all that were in the ark. Paul speaks of "the care of all the churches" (2 Cor 11:28). Noah could, in picture, say the same.

The evangelist is seen in 1 Timothy 1, the teacher in 1 Timothy 4 and the pastor in 1 Timothy 3. However the thought of care runs throughout the pastoral epistles, such as hospital care for "those who are doting or sick" (1 Tim 6:4 RV). Another concept is that of the school, suggested by the many references to "teaching". Besides all these, the family circle is seen in the instruction to widows and their families in 1 Timothy 5, and behaviour and order in the house of God in 1 Timothy 3.

The three great gifts in operation today are the evangelist, the teacher and the pastor, and are all seen in figure in Noah in Genesis 6. May the Lord raise up many to meet the great need of this day.

This brings to an end our consideration of the manifestation of the Lord in chapter 6 of Genesis. No doubt careful study will yield further treasures to the Bible student, for the Word is so full. We can all bring our little vessels to this magnificent chapter and draw of its fulness, and still there is an abundance left.

24

THE GOODNESS AND SEVERITY OF GOD

Genesis chapter 7 contains the record of the flood, and the mercy of God displayed in the deliverance of Noah and his family. An apt title would be "The goodness and severity of God", the words being borrowed from Romans 11:22.

"The Lord said unto Noah, Come thou and all thy house into the ark; for thee have I seen righteous before me in this generation" (v. 1). The word God used was "Come" not "Go", so the Lord was already in the ark and was calling Noah to Himself. He had gone before, He was leading the way. So it was with the experience of Moses at the burning bush. The Lord said, "I have seen... I have heard", the Lord was there in the midst of the people, and now was about to send Moses. This can be seen in a greater way in the wilderness journey. The Lord went before in the pillar of cloud by day and of fire by night. All that the people of Israel passed through the Lord had been there first. Again, in crossing the Jordan the ark of the covenant went before them into the waters of the river and the people followed. All this points to the Lord Jesus, who walked through this wilderness of a world before us as we do now. He is the Pioneer in the epistle to the Hebrews, One that has blazed the trail, the Captain of our salvation, the One that goes in front, and has made clear the path for others to follow. This qualifies Him to be the great High Priest of His people, which is

NOAH

the main reason for His manhood. "Though he were a Son, yet learned he obedience by the things which he suffered" (Heb 5:8). It was not that the Lord needed to learn to obey, He was always obedient, the meaning is rather that in His experience as a man, He learned the cost of obedience, and obedience to God always involves cost in some way. In this we follow His steps (1 Pet 2:21), enduring patiently the suffering that sometimes comes by reason of obedience to the will of God.

The Lord Jesus then has gone before:

1. To qualify him to be our great High Priest.
2. To be our example.
3. To encourage us in any affliction we have to face.

To the suffering church at Smyrna, the Lord presented Himself as the One who was dead and is now alive, so suitable to those dear believers who were facing death because of their faith. The Lord would encourage them, "Fear none of those things". He was in prison just as they were; He suffered of the Jews as they did; He was tested by the devil as they were experiencing; He entered into a violent death as they were called to enter. But He is alive; death is not the end; rather is it the beginning of glory; they shall live also; the crown of life is promised them. God went first into the ark.

Again, note what it was that attracted God, the righteous life of Noah, "Thee have I seen righteous before me in this generation". It is godliness that is so acceptable in the sight of the Lord, not gift or ability as some are inclined to think. After all, such gift is given by the Lord to believers as a stewardship to use for His glory. The same could be said about prosperity, and all the other good things which the Lord showers upon men, "what hast thou that thou didst not receive?" (1 Cor

THE GOODNESS AND SEVERITY OF GOD

4:7). All such blessing, whether material or spiritual, makes the recipient more responsible to the Lord. Yet the Lord looks with favour upon the righteous life. Noah could have delivered himself because of his righteous character (Ezek 14:14) if he had lived in Jerusalem at the time of the ministry of Ezekiel. The fathers trusted in God and were delivered (Ps 22:4) no doubt because of their faith and righteousness. The silent years of the life of our Lord upon the earth were well pleasing to God, as was expressed by the opened heaven and the voice when He was baptized. Until this time, no miracle had been performed, no ministry had been given; the secret life of righteousness, lived in obscurity, was infinitely precious to God. It is so with every child of God; the righteous life can avail much, even in prayer as James informs us (James 5:16). To this could be added the words of Peter, "The eyes of the Lord are over the righteous, and his ears are open unto their prayers" (1 Pet 3:12), quoting from Psalm 34:15. Noah had this testimony from the mouth of God Himself, "Thee have I found righteous before me in this generation". This testimony shines out all the more when one considers the dark background of the corruption and violence of that day. To all that profess Christ, Paul extends the exhortation, "Godliness is profitable unto all things, having promise of the life that now is, and of that which is to come" (1 Tim 4:8). How wonderful the statement, "God shut him in" (Gen 7:16). Noah did not have to close the door after himself, he just went in, and all that were with him, and God closed the door. We can rest assured that the door was very secure, there was absolute safety in the ark. Security here must have been most encouraging, Noah was depending on the power, the faithfulness, and the work that God Himself had performed. From the least to the greatest security in

NOAH

Christ Jesus is so comforting to the believer. He has finished the work, He has the power to save, He abides faithful. If a soul enters by faith the Lord does the rest, all is secure. These opening verses therefore present God in a very encouraging way undoubtedly setting forth the invitation to enter, and the strong security for all that do so. A faithful God could only act so.

God's power in creation is now seen. God is over all seasons and times. The number of the days is determined beforehand. "Yet seven days, and I will cause it to rain upon the earth forty days and forty nights" (v. 4). "It came to pass after seven days, that the waters of the flood were upon the earth" (v. 10). "The rain was upon the earth forty days and forty nights" (v.12). All was as the Lord predicted. Quite a series of days are recorded in the sequel to the flood, and all were appointed by the Lord beforehand.

As well as the seven and forty days there are also the one hundred and fifty days that the waters were upon the earth after the rain ceased (v. 24). This seems to mean that the mountains were covered during that time. After those days the ark rested upon Mount Ararat (8:3-4), in other words, the top parts of the mountains appeared. Forty days later Noah opened the window and sent forth the raven and the dove (8:6). The raven did not return but the dove came back to the ark again. Seven days later the dove was sent out again, but returned. Then after another seven days he sent out the dove for the third time, and it did not return. When the word of the Lord came, "Go forth of the ark", Noah obeyed; he would not move without a word from the Lord. This series of days is bound to be significant, especially those at the first: the seven, the forty, the one hundred and fifty, and the forty. Each day was predetermined by the Lord. It is ever so, the great tribulation is determined by the Lord to last 1260 days (Rev 12:6), not one day more nor one less. All is measured by the Lord. There are two short periods of times predicted in the prophetic Word. Both are most important, and both are very short in comparison to the other great time periods of prophecy. These are, the period of the public ministry of the true Christ as seen in the Gospels, and that of the false Christ yet to come. Both are three and a half years in duration. For every day of rejection of the true Christ, Israel shall taste of a day of suffering under the false Christ. They lived by the law, an eye for an eye, and God shall deal with them after that law.

If the Lord had predetermined that the great tribulation should be longer than 1260 days, then no flesh would be saved; man would completely destroy himself, and none would remain (Matt 24:22). How terrible and violent those days will be, as the Lord is not speaking of spiritual salvation but of physical life.

The millennium will last 1000 years, and the duration of the time of grace now enjoyed is predetermined by heaven. All this is seen in the Lord's dealings in the flood in these important chapters. Has not the Lord planned our lives in the same intimate way? Concerning Paul it is said, "he is a chosen vessel unto me", and to Peter the Lord gave the keys of the kingdom. Surely it is true of ourselves that the Lord has a purpose and is working according to a pattern in our lives. The length of that work and testimony in our experience is all planned by the Lord. This thought is borne out also in the temptation of our Lord, "Man shall not live by bread alone, but by every word that proceedeth out of the mouth of God" (Matt 4:4). Not bread nor the lack of it determines the length of a man's life, rather the word spoken by the mouth of God. When the Lord says so, the life is finished. The rich farmer of Luke 12 was planning for the future, but God said, "Thou fool, this night thy soul shall be

NOAH

required of thee". The man died that night; his life depended upon the word of God, not on possessions and earthy plans. The same was the experience of Hezekiah in the opposite way. The word came to him, "Set thine house in order; for thou shalt die, and not live" (2 Kings 20:1). The man prayed, and the word of the Lord came again; fifteen years had been added to his life. Our times, experiences and trials are governed by the plan of God for us, and the person who exercises faith leaves all in His hands: He holds the future.

Next there is a tremendous display of the wrath and severity of God, the terrible flood upon the ungodly. A great part of the chapter is taken up with this (vv. 17-24), and none can escape except those in the ark. Consider a few remarks about this first clear record of the wrath and righteous judgment of the Lord.

It was exactly just as the Lord had said in the earlier verses. The word of the Lord cannot pass away; it is easier for heaven and earth to pass away than the word of the Lord; it will never fail (Matt 5:18). A host of Bible passages foretell the destruction of the earth by fire, such as 2 Peter 3 already considered in a previous chapter, and it shall come to pass; nothing can frustrate the purposes of God. Men will say, "where is the promise of his coming", but the day of the Lord shall come as a thief in the night; the world shall be taken unawares. So future judgments are as sure as those that are past, for the word of the Lord must stand.

Not one escaped, all flesh died (v. 21). "All in whose nostrils was the breath of life, of all that was in the dry land, died" (v. 22). "Every living substance was destroyed" (v. 23). "Noah only remained alive, and they that were with him in the ark" (v. 23). All perished: "the flood came and took them all away" was the comment of the Lord in Matt 24.

THE GOODNESS AND SEVERITY OF GOD

Salvation is also seen, but only for some, namely those in the ark. Salvation is of the Lord and is obtained only in His way, there is no other. Likewise, the man in Christ shall not come into judgment but is passed from death unto life. The sinner has no merit, all is the work of the Saviour.

His works are ever complete, even that of judgment. Nothing is left unfinished.

Nothing is out of control. This has already been considered. The very days and the length of time the waters were upon the earth were all controlled by the Lord. Man does things, invents weapons etc. but then things soon get out of control, not so with the Lord, all is ordered by his hand.

There was no repentance with the Lord in His judgment. As man refused to repent so there was none with the Lord. This work of wrath had to be, His holy nature was in accord with it. God repented that he had made man, but did not repent of the judgment of the flood brought upon man.

Finally, the Lord used a natural element, water. The next time He will use fire, probably the atomic energy that has been present in the universe all the time. Man has now discovered it. God placed it there and will no doubt use it even to the passing away of the present earth in His own time.

Genesis 7 then is an important passage dealing with the subject of the goodness of God in saving Noah, and the severity of God in the judgment of the then world. A very searching passage indeed.

25

THE FAITHFUL CREATOR
IN GENESIS 8

The faithfulness of the Lord shines out in the whole of chapter 8, first to Noah, "And God remembered Noah, and every living thing, and all the cattle that was with him in the ark" (v.1). How beautiful is God's consideration for the brute creation as seen in this verse. Later, the law of Moses concerned not only the well being of man, but also that of the domestic beast. The law demanded that a man must not ill-treat his beast but rather to care for it. The close of the chapter widens out to all creation: "While the earth remaineth, seedtime and harvest, and cold and heat, and summer and winter, and day and night shall not cease" (v. 22). Here undoubtedly is the faithfulness of God as Creator. On reflection, Noah could have told later of the goodness of God to him, to those with him, and to all the earth, of which we now enjoy the fulness. All this comes from the hand of the faithful Creator.

Verse 1 is a great consolation to the people of God: His eye was upon His people. God remembered Noah, though the huge ark and the man in it were so small upon the vast waters of the flood. In the midst of the terrible judgment brought about by the hand of the Lord, yet His eye was upon His people, those that had made a covenant with Him by sacrifice. This thought is similar to John 13:1. Jesus knew that His hour was come, that He should depart out of the world unto the Father, having loved His own which were in the world, He loved them to the uttermost. He was occupied with His own rather than with the great ordeal of the cross that was before Him. In fact, all the suffering of the cross was for them. The word "uttermost" is a reference to that cross with all its suffering and shame. Note, "his own which were in the world". He had many saints in heaven, but they were safe. These others were in the hostile world, and He remembered them. Yes, God remembered Noah. The same can be said of the 144000 of the book of Revelation. They will be brought through the tribulation, and not one of them will be lost in spite of all the powers of detection that the Beast and his followers can muster. God remembers them. Eventually they appear on Mount Sion with the Lord. All the sore tribulation is passed, and they enter into the eternal kingdom of our Lord. They will be able to tell something of the faithfulness of the Lord.

Again creation must obey the Lord, "God made a wind to pass over the earth, and the waters were assuaged" (v. 1). It must have been a warm wind so as to evaporate the waters. The Lord sent an east wind to divide the waters of the Red Sea (Exod 14). The winds are at His command. The book of Revelation speaks of angels holding back the winds of the earth. While this no doubt is symbolic, yet the Lord can command the winds. He also rebuked the wind while on the boat, and there was a great calm. All things created must obey Him, "for thy pleasure they are and were created" (Rev 4:11). In the matter of the flood, He controlled the rains and the fountains of the deep to bring forth the waters of the flood, now He makes them to cease (v. 2). All things are in His hand to use as He wills, and to fulfil His will for the times and for His people.

185

NOAH

Note also that the Lord accomplishes things progressively, here over a period of 150 days before the top of the mountains appeared, "the waters returned from off the earth continually" (v. 3). God cannot be hurried in His work, but He goes on steadily, progressively. This is a principle with the Lord stamped upon the very first chapter of the Bible. In Genesis 1 the Lord did some work each day over the period of six days. Now no doubt the Lord could have accomplished all in one day, that we fully believe, but to do so was not His way. So with the great subject of revelation. All was not revealed in a short time, rather over a period of 1500 years or so. But God completed the revelation, now we have all the Word of God. The principle is relevant in our lives. We are so small and insignificant among the masses of humanity, but the eye of the Lord is upon us. He is at work in our lives. We exist for Him. Peter in the Gospels is a clear illustration of how the Lord trained him for his future apostleship. The school of God, as we call it, is well illustrated in the story of Jacob, and even more so in the tragic yet wonderful story of Joseph. The Lord is working progressively in the life of every believer.

We know from Peter that the Lord waited with much longsuffering in those far off days (1 Pet 3:20), but eventually the flood came. God can be neither hurried nor hindered in the work He is doing, and that is a great solace to the child of faith.

Again, God finished His work. Nothing is ever left incomplete. This is one of the great central truths of the Word. The Lord not only washed the disciples' feet, but He also dried them with the towel with which He was girded: He finished the task, He did not leave them with wet feet. It is so in this passage, "behold the face of the ground was *dry,* and, in the second month on the seven and twentieth day of the month, was the earth *dried*"

(vv. 13-14). Noah likely did not even get his feet wet. What God does, He does properly and completely. In like manner the people of Israel crossed the Red Sea on dry land, and the same can be said of the crossing of Jordan.

There is a deep significance in the resting of the ark upon the mount. Note the date, the seventeenth day of the seventh month. Now the passover was on the fourteenth day of the first month, a type of the death of our Lord. Three days later He arose from the dead, that is on the seventeenth day. The ark resting on that date is a figure of His resurrection. The ark therefore is a type of the death of Christ for our sins, and our shelter in Him, and the resting on the mount of His resurrection. It is interesting that it was upon a mountain that the Lord appeared to His disciples in Matt 28, when He said, "All power is given unto me in heaven and in earth". How suitable is the picture here of that great day.

The chapter is in two distinct parts. In verses 1-14 Noah is inside the ark and verses 15-22 would be outside the ark. This second section contains much precious instruction.

The Lord did not give the command to leave the ark until it was safe to do so. The ground is mentioned as being dry in verses 12-13 before the command to leave came. The ark was a safe place in the storm, but now the calm had come. Noah was not stepping into mud or anything uncomfortable. Surely this is a wonderful example of the consideration of the Lord for His own. This lovely thoughtfulness of the Lord is illustrated in Matt 4. John the Baptist was cast into prison. Not until then did the Lord call unto Himself the disciples that were formerly John's. While John was a free man he needed these disciples, but when he was in prison, never to be free again, he no longer needed them. At that

NOAH

point the Lord called them to Himself. If the Lord had done this while John was free he would have been perplexed. The Lord would not do such a thing, He considered the feelings of His servant John.

The altar of Noah is paramount in the chapter. This altar has been dealt with in a previous chapter, but it must be studied from God's point of view. The response of the man brought great delight to the Lord. Of course this was God's intention when He commanded Noah to take seven pairs of the clean animals into the ark (Gen 7:2-3). It is wonderful when man fulfils the intention of God in such things. There was no recorded word that Noah was to offer. The offerings proved to be delightful to God, as was also the quick response of the man. This can be well applied to ourselves: the spiritual and material sacrifices were no doubt the intention of God, and should be offered spontaneously. How marvellous it is that puny man upon the earth can give to God who possess heaven and earth, who owns the cattle on the thousand hills, and that He is willing to receive from our hands. Verse 21 refers to a sweet savour. This is the first occurrence in the Scriptures of this kind of offering, which later is developed in Leviticus. Noah was original in a number of things, such as the altar, the vineyard and the wine and here is another original matter. It would seem that our gifts are a sweet savour unto the Lord; even Paul's preaching of the gospel was: "we are unto God a sweet savour of Christ" (2 Cor 2:15).

The offerings were of the clean animals. This is the quality the Lord requires and is in keeping with His holy nature. All must be clean. The Psalms insist on this, "who shall ascend into the hill of the Lord?... He that hath clean hands" (Ps 24:3-4).

Again, in the prayer meeting Paul exhorts that the men that pray lift up holy hands (1 Tim 2:8). "Be ye clean, that bear the vessels of the Lord" is the exhortation of Isa 52:11. On the strength of this it is good to give to the Lord, but to give only of the best and of the clean, not as those of Israel who offered that which had blemish, the blind, the lame and the sick (Mal 1:8).

The closing verses are often quoted. Here is the faithful Creator most certainly, flowing out from the household of Noah to the vastness of the earth and heaven. God controls the seasons as well as the rains and winds as seen earlier. The farmer, and all who partake of the produce of the earth, are indebted to the Lord who has ordained the laws of nature. The curse was not removed here, rather it was lessened. The earth was to yield to cultivation. But the curse will be completely removed in the millennium: "There shall be no more curse" (Rev 22:3).

The great promise of God recorded here is important: He will not smite the earth again by means of water (v. 21). This is emphasised again in 9:11. The Lord will smite the earth again, but with fire not with water. With this agrees the ministry of John the Baptist, speaking of the Christ, "He shall baptise in fire", no doubt a reference to the coming judgment when the earth shall be engulfed with fire.

The verses at the close of the chapter are most beautiful, and all depend upon these faithful words for their daily living. The four couplets are most interesting, teaching us that things will continue. True, there is famine at times but not on a world scale. One place is empty, the other is full. It can only be so in the light of this promise. In spiritual things also the same principles surely apply.

Seedtime and harvest: The labour of sowing is bound to yield a harvest eventually. Sometimes much sowing seems to bring forth nothing, but the harvest shall surely come, and all shall have a reward (John 4:36). This is very cheering for the evangelist.

Cold and heat: We do not always experience the mild south wind of blessing, but also the chilling north or east winds of trial and testing. However, the cold is as necessary as the heat to make one mature in the school of God.

Summer and winter: Both can make us prepare and both present an opportunity to service. The virtuous woman of Prov 31 was able to work in winter and summer; harvest fields yield to her touch and her children are clothed in time of snow. As Paul would exhort, "Be instant in season and out of season" (2 Tim 4:2). Note that summer comes before winter in this couplet, whereas cold comes before heat in the previous. In experience, blessing sometimes precedes famine as in the case of Egypt. Again, sometimes the cold experience of trouble yields the peaceable fruits afterward, as in the case of Job.

Day and night would suggest opportunities. "Walk in the day", is the exhortation of the Lord (John 11:9); "Do not sleep in the day", Paul exhorts (1 Thess 5:6-7). On the other hand the apostle Paul speaks of praying in the night in 2 Tim 1:3. He certainly did so in the jail with Silas in Acts 16. Opportunities are there by day and night, and one needs to buy them up, and not to miss them.

All these contain great lessons for the child of God. Every cloud has a silver lining, but every silver lining has a cloud. Both blessing and reproach are necessary to furnish maturity. The successive seasons were to bring forth the fruit of the earth, and in a similar way the believer with these experiences brings forth fruit to God.

One little point will bring to a close this chapter. The things that God has joined together we must acknowledge. Seedtime and harvest, cold and heat, summer and winter, day and night are opposites, yet they work together. The most significant couplet in the chapter is in verse 16: Thou and thy wife, thy sons and thy sons' wives with thee. Marriage is established by the Lord, and He expects married couples to be together in all things. Even those of opposite temperament can work successfully together. A beautiful example of husband and wife working together is Aquila and Priscilla. May it ever be so with the people of God.

26

THE GOD OF ALL GRACE IN GENESIS 9

Chapter nine falls into two distinct parts, and what a contrast in material there is between the two parts.

1. God and His ways: the wonderful covenant He makes with all flesh (vv. 1-17).
2. Noah and his ways: he falls into drunkenness (vv. 18-29).

The covenant of God ends in blessing to all, the failure of Noah ends with a curse to a third of his posterity. Part one sees government passing into the hands of men, the beginning of human responsibility to guard the rights of others. Part two shows man's failure to govern himself, the lack of self control. It is always the same: man will seek to control others but cannot control himself. The Lord speaks of the man who would cast the speck of sawdust out of his brother's eye while a log of wood is protruding from his own eye, so his vision is impaired (Matt 7:1). The Pharisees were blind leaders of the blind, and it is sadly the case in some churches that those responsible for leadership are ready to judge others but have not the moral right to do so. Such is the nature of man: failure is all too common.

The first section is the focal point of this chapter; it unfolds the wonderful display of the grace of God: His covenant, His interest in the well being and rights of man, and his prescription to preserve the sanctity of life. The section concerning food relates to the sustenance of man upon the earth.

This is followed by the everlasting covenant that God makes with all flesh (vv. 8-17), a forerunner of the new covenant based upon the blood of Christ that brings man into the spiritual relationship with God. These two covenants together manifest the grace of God towards men, the first providing for the temporal things, as it brings forward material blessing, the latter providing spiritually and eternally. The material blessings the Lord gives freely to all mankind because they are of the earth, the seed of Adam, that life may be sustained and in a measure made pleasant. The eternal blessing too makes happy, but only those who are under the headship of Christ. The two heads can be examined in Romans 5, and 1 Corinthians 15. Again, there are two spheres found in Colossians 1. The Lord is the firstborn of all creation, that is of the material creation: He made all and controls all. His primacy in the spiritual realm is seen in the firstborn from the dead: of all that are on the resurrection side, Christ is the firstborn, that is the holder of chief place. Firstborn in Scripture always has to do with rank, whereas first fruits have to do with time and order. In both realms Christ has the chief place; all comes through Him.

The clear distinction between these two paragraphs in the section can be seen in the introduction to each: God blessed Noah (v.1); God said to Noah (v.8). A different idea is presented in each: in the first, man's responsibility to govern, and the provision for life's support; in the second the part the Lord plays in the everlasting covenant, He will not destroy the earth again in a flood. Both are similar in outcome: the good of man; and both end on the same note: the earth being populated (v. 7); and God's covenant with all flesh, no matter how many (v. 17). This teaches us that God is no respecter of persons.

While we have commenced our commentary at verse 1 the subject really commences in 8:20 and continues to verse 17 of this chapter. There the Lord announces "I will not again curse the ground ... neither will I again smite any more every living thing"; there cannot be another universal judgment by water. This is followed by the lovely words "seedtime and harvest, and cold and heat, summer and winter, and day and night, shall not cease". From there on to this ninth chapter all is a new way of life for man, under a covenant from the Lord. How true in the spiritual realm; the believer shall not come into judgment but is passed from death unto life (John 5:24). He has delivered us from the power of darkness and has translated us into the kingdom of the Son of His love. The risen Lord expresses it thus to Paul, "To turn them from darkness to light, and from the power of Satan unto God, that they may receive forgiveness of sins, and inheritance among them that are sanctified" (Acts 26:18).

The material in verses 1-7 highlights five things necessary to maintain life upon the earth.

People are to be multiplied. In chapter 10 this develops into the division of the nations, and out of these God would later call a people for His Name to inherit heaven. Man has to populate the earth and subdue it. This makes way for all discoveries and scientific advancement that have made life more intelligent and pleasant.

Man is to be supreme over the earth; he is to conquer, advance and discover. The fear of him shall be upon every beast of the field and every fowl of the air. When one considers this, how far man has come. The discoveries are legion and continually new things are coming to light. This is because of the intelligence God has given to man. Man was created in the image of God, and for His enjoyment. This was the purpose of God, and why government was placed in the hands of man from this point in history. The writer of Psalm 8 marvels at this mercy and says, "What is man, that thou art mindful of him? and the son of man, that thou visitest him?" He is referring to the works of God which are all for the good of mankind.

Alas, man has fallen in sin and has not the moral fitness to rule over the whole earth. Many have tried to do so and have failed. The eternal Son became man for this purpose among others, that He should reign and subject all under his feet. All will be subject to the perfect man Jesus.

Until this time man was a vegetarian, now meats are permissible in his diet. Whether it had never entered into the thoughts of man to eat meat or he knew it was prohibited, we do not know. However, from this point man is permitted to eat meat as well as the fruits of the earth. Later, Israel had to make a distinction between clean and unclean in beasts, fish and birds (Lev 11) because they were a separated nation. Besides, God was interested in the health of the nation. In the New Testament all meats are again acceptable, "every creature of God is good, and nothing to be refused, if it be received with thanksgiving" (1 Tim 4:4). Noah was able to distinguish between clean and unclean in the sacrifices he offered. Many people have reverted to a vegetarian diet on health grounds. It is permissible to abstain from meat as a health consideration, but to do so on religious grounds is to set aside the Word of God as found in 1 Tim 4:4. This passage is not suggesting that all meats are good for the body. It rather warns against abstaining from such as a means to spiritual experience as in the previous verse. Certain were forbidding to marry, and commanding to abstain from meats which God created to be received with thanksgiving, a clear reference to Genesis 9:3.

While meat was allowed, blood was not. The life is in the blood (v. 4) and so it is prohibited. It can already be seen in the early chapters of Genesis that blood is the only way to approach God. Cain refused a blood sacrifice and was rejected. Abel offered to God a more excellent sacrifice than Cain; his offering involved the shedding of blood, the yielding up of a life. Also, Noah's burnt offerings were all sweet savours to the Lord. These, with what were to follow in the Levitical sacrifices, were signposts pointing to that great sacrifice of the Lamb of Calvary. Abstaining from eating blood is one of the points of the law of Moses that were binding upon man long before the law of Moses came into existence.

The final thing was the inauguration of the death penalty. Again it was a command that predated the law of Moses. This is the chief point in the revelation given here; this is where human government really came in, making man responsible for maintaining the sanctity of life: the crime of murder should be punished by death. God required blood for blood, even when an animal was involved. Man was the servant of God in this matter to see that it was carried out. It was always the intention of God that man should obey His ways and laws. They were all for the good of man, and for the glory of God. It is so with the Christian today. The angels are largely passed by in this dispensation; the believer is the channel of God's ways to forward blessing to all. He is the Lord, and every believer is a servant to the Lord, to do His will.

Human government is commented upon in Romans 13. There must be the government of the people or else all is confusion and anarchy. God will have order in His creation. Christians above all others should acknowledge this. Romans 13 is very important especially to the Lord's people.

The governments of men are called "the higher powers", the powers that are ordained of God. Their mandate is from above, they are responsible before God to see that justice is done for all without respect of persons.

They are also called "the powers that be", they exist as ordered by God for the good of mankind.

Again, they are called "the ordinance of God" as ordained by God, so to resist them is to resist God Himself.

"Rulers" is another way in which they are described, the Lord has placed authority in their hands. Power is on their side to punish evil and to reward good.

Finally they are called "the ministers of God", as doing God service in maintaining order in His creation, specifically preserving the sanctity of life. The sword is the symbol of this power.

The believer above all people must be subject to these powers. This lies along the principle of Christian righteousness. Now all this stems from this chapter in Genesis. Up until this time God punished the offender as in the case of Cain, and of Lamech whose posterity perished in the flood. But from this point in human history that responsibility rests with man.

The order of these requirements is in the form of inverted parallels as follows.

A. Populate the earth. Verse 1
  B. Fear of you, authority over the beasts. Verse 2
    C. Eat flesh. Verse 3
    C. Do not eat the blood. Verse 4
  B. Fear, authority in human sphere. Verses 5-6
A. Populate the earth. Verse 7.
  All is for the good of the human race, to bless them

and yet to control them so that order would prevail. The family and the nations are of God, and His interest is with the sons of men.

Two points here are worthy of note. When a government brings in laws contrary to the laws of God, then the believer must resist. Peter made this clear, "We ought to obey God rather than men" (Acts 5:29). If the government of any country runs contrary to God's word, and to obey an injunction would involve disobedience to the Lord, then the clear duty of the believer is to refuse.

The other thing to remember is that the government of God is superimposed upon the governments of men. If they violate the laws of God, as in this chapter and elsewhere, then the Lord Himself steps in with judgment. Such was the case with Israel. They declined into idolatry, neglected the widows and poor, and persecuted the prophets of the Lord, so the land spewed them out (Lev 18:28). Also in the history of Babylon, that great nation was put down because it sorely afflicted Israel and other nations, and abused the government placed into their hands by God. It is always so, and the past wars are a witness to this sober principle.

The setting aside of the laws and forms of government delineated in these first seven verses issues in confusion and increased crime, the terrible canker seen among the nations of today. While this particular dispensation ended with Genesis 11, yet the principles are still binding as seen from Romans 13 as regards government, and 1 Timothy 4 as touching food.

27

THE EVERLASTING COVENANT

The second section of Genesis 9 deals with the covenant the Lord made with all flesh (vv. 8-17). Thus, there are two covenants passed on to Noah. First, that of chapter 6:18 in the context of judgment upon that generation. The covenant was one of salvation to Noah. The Lord said, "With thee will I establish my covenant: and thou shalt come into the ark" (v. 18). Safety was in the ark. The covenant meant death to some and life to others. This therefore was a temporary covenant and no longer applies, except in type as found in the Lord Jesus. However the covenant in Genesis 9 appears as an "everlasting covenant" and so applies today, and to all flesh. Let us now consider the details of this everlasting covenant.

It is mentioned seven times. Now this is the number of completeness, an indication of its importance. The works of the Lord are perfect, and this covenant bears that mark.

It is not a covenant entered into by two parties as is general, but rather it is one sided. It issues from the promise of God, and is not dependent on human merits, nor on the faithfulness of man.

Contrast this with the covenant made with Israel at Sinai. The people were responsible to keep the laws, and God was responsible to bless them if they did. Man is not placed in responsibility here.

199

NOAH

The covenant is made with all flesh, even the beasts of the field: "every living thing" (v.10). It is not a question of salvation as in Genesis 6:18 where the covenant was with Noah unto salvation from the destruction of the flood.

It is everlasting (v. 16), so it will remain until the end of time. Different epochs may pass by in which God deals with man in different ways, but this will remain unchanged.

The pledge of the covenant is that never again will the Lord destroy the earth by a flood. There will be judgments many, but never a universal flood to destroy. At times there have been devastating floods in certain areas of the earth, but these were local and have to do with the discipline of the nation in question. Again, God often judges by the withholding of water and the inevitable famines that follow. The covenant states therefore that God will never again bring a world wide catastrophe by means of water.

The token of this covenant is the bow in the sky, so when anyone sees the rainbow he is reminded of the faithfulness of our covenant keeping God.

This covenant issues out of the sacrifice of 8:21. The Lord smelled the sweet savour and said in His heart, "I will not again curse the ground any more for man's sake (that is curse by the flood of waters); for the imagination of man's heart is evil from his youth: neither will I again smite any more every thing living, as I have done". The Lord shall again smite in judgment, but with fire not with water as is made clear in the New Testament.

Later in the history of Israel the Lord speaks of a new covenant made with the house of Israel (Jer 31:31-4). This is explained in Hebrews 8 as being the result of the death of Christ. Now the features of the new covenant are similar to those of the covenant in our chapter.

THE EVERLASTING COVENANT

Comparisons can profitably be made between them.

It is perfect, and fulfils all the shadows and types of the Old Testament. It will never give place to another as indicated in Hebrews 8. The old covenant of the law of Moses passed away because of its imperfection, but this is perfect and complete.

The new covenant is again unilateral and unconditional, "I will make a new covenant... I will put my laws into their mind, and write them in their hearts...all shall know me, from the least to the greatest" (Heb 8:8-11). It is so different from the old in which the people were responsible to keep the laws in their own strength. Now there will be power indwelling to enable them to do so, a one party covenant, "Not by works of righteousness which we have done, but according to his mercy he saved us" (Titus 3:5).

As the covenant here involved all the people of earth, so the new covenant involves all the people of God, all that believe, and the assurance is given to all such. In Adam all sinned; there is no difference; all born into this world are naturally under the headship of Adam. In the same way, those who are born again are under the headship of Christ, and all live in Him irrespective of their spiritual capacity or condition.

Both covenants are everlasting. Hebrews 13:25 speaks of the sacrifice of Christ as being the blood of the everlasting covenant.

The pledge of the covenant is, "Their sins and their iniquities will I remember no more forever".

The token or sign of the new covenant is the Spirit. He indwells the believer and changes the life that all may see His power to make one different from those that perish.

Both covenants are based upon sacrifice, the one on Noah's offerings, the other on the one great sacrifice of

201

NOAH

whom they speak, that of Christ. All is summed up beautifully as "the blood of the everlasting covenant" (Heb 13:25). It would appear that the everlasting covenant of Genesis 9 is a forerunner of that of which Hebrews speaks, and is the opposite of the covenant of law. The law of Moses was based upon works, which fallen man was powerless to perform, but this covenant with Noah spoke of the better things to come.

The Lord would have us take particular note of the contrast between this covenant and that of the law of Moses which came later. That law depended upon the works of man, all was the responsibility of man in the flesh, but this covenant depended entirely upon God Himself. Note the constant use of the pronoun "I". It occurs twice in verse 9: "And I, behold, I establish".

Again: "I will establish" (v. 11).

"The covenant which I make" (v. 12).

"I do set my bow in the sky" (v. 13).

"When I bring a cloud over the earth" (v.14).

"I will remember my covenant" (v. 15).

Twice in verse 16. "I will look upon it, that I may remember".

Finally, "The token of the covenant, which I have established" (v.17).

The pronoun "I" appears a total of ten times; this is most significant. When the ten commandments were given, ten times over God said, "*Thou* shalt" or "*Thou shalt not*". God takes all responsibility here, but the law placed the responsibility entirely upon man. The same thought is noticed in the features of the new covenant, where nine times God is presented by the majestic "I". All is of God, all is sovereign grace (Heb 8:8-12).

It is beautiful to see that in the covenant of judgment in chapter 6, when the Lord announces the judgment of the flood, He uses the pronoun "I" six times. This indicates two things: first that God is more ready to bless than to judge. He uses the personal pronoun ten times in blessing and six times in judgment. Second, six is the number of man, and the Lord links this with the judgment he deserves.

While the covenants of Genesis 9 and Hebrews 8 are similar in their features, yet there is a major difference. One has to do with life upon the present earth, the other with life upon the new earth; one is natural, the other is spiritual; one relates to this world, and the other to the world to come. Of course, this first is a picture of that which is to come, and the last was first in the mind of God.

The two sections of Genesis 9 blend beautifully. Verses 1-7 are temporal, verses 8-17 are everlasting, and typical of the spiritual blessing to come. God takes care of both temporal and eternal, natural and spiritual. These two things are often classed together in Scripture. An example is found in Genesis 2-3: in chapter 2 the providence of God provides all things necessary to maintain natural life, but in chapter 3 redemption is promised in the seed of the woman when the fall of man had taken place. Colossians 1 also brings the two thoughts together, speaking of Christ as the first-born of all creation, and the first-born from the dead, those who stand on resurrection ground. He is the source of all created things, so He has the pre-eminence in that sphere; He also made peace by the blood of His cross, making Him to be superior in the spiritual realm as well. This is what is meant by "in all things he might have the pre-eminence". These two again are put in another form in Hebrews 1:2-3. God has appointed Him to be heir of all things by whom also He made the ages: the natural realm; having made purification for sins: the spiritual realm. It is of great comfort that the Lord looks after His own by meeting their need in time as in the first verse of this chapter, and also their eternal need as in type in this covenant.

The faithfulness of God is seen in the bow. It is again found in Revelation 4 surrounding the throne of God. There the praise is unto the Lord first for creation (Rev 4), and then redemption (Rev 5). In Genesis 9 the bow is for the eye of man, but in Revelation 4 it is around the throne for the eyes of those in heaven. God is faithful and true, and this brings wonderful assurance to those who believe. Greater still is the assurance derived from the permanence of the covenant. It was based only upon the blood of animals, but the new and everlasting covenant is based upon better sacrifices, even the blood of Christ, God's perfect Son. If God is faithful to the creatures of His hand in this passage, how much more to those who are born again and partakers of the divine nature. How reassuring it is to read Romans 5 in which the Spirit uses the phrase "much more" five times. Paul is speaking of the trespass offering, and pointing out that the believer has gained much more in Christ than ever he lost in Adam.

Consider now the last section of Genesis 9, the failure of Noah and its consequences. This subject has already been dealt with in the chapter of *Noah the Man*, but must be contemplated again to see further manifestation of the Lord in the passage.

As there are many who miss the new covenant and come into grief, so here after the teaching about the covenant, the final part of the chapter speaks of a curse, judgment instead of blessing as so often admonished of in the "warning passages" in Hebrews. Ham was not as sincere as his brothers, he was not affectionately attached to his father as they were. Ham saw the nakedness of his drunken father inside the tent, and went out and told his brethren. It would seem that at the very least Ham gloated over the nakedness of his father; something more sinister may be implied in the wording. At any rate, he acted neither with courtesy nor discretion; obviously he had no concern for the old man. He is no doubt a picture of Israel. Saved from the corruption of the world, they followed Christ to a degree outwardly, but never really left the old Judaism and so placed themselves under the curse (Heb 6:8). Even in the wilderness they disobeyed, and God swore in His wrath that they would not enter into the land (Heb 3:11). Because of their unbelief they are still under the curse of the law (Gal 3:10-11). Shem and Japheth took a garment, laid it upon their shoulders, and went backward and covered the nakedness of their father. They acted out of reverence and respect and obtained the blessing.

Ham likely considered his father a foolish old man not worthy of attention, and had no respect for the revelation of God that was given through him. In a way he could be considered as one of those who "neglect so great salvation" (Heb 2:3).

The chapter closes with God's division of the nations. He is in control and sets their bounds in the next chapter, but the interrelationships of the main tributaries also appear at the close of this chapter.

From Ham sprang Canaan, then Babylon. Both in turn were conquered, Canaan by Israel, and Babylon by the Medes and Persians. Ham cannot hold his position. Many appear to have this failure, even some gifted among the people of God.

Japheth produced the king of the north as found in Ezekiel 38-9, the Germany of the past, and will produce the future king of the north that shall figure so much in the last days. He also was conquered in the past, and shall be in the future although "enlarged" (v. 27). Japheth

NOAH

has a large part in God's plan during *the times of the Gentiles.*

Shem was to produce Israel and the Messiah. This is the important line and in chapter 11 is traced to Abraham. Note the wording, "Blessed be the Lord God of Shem" (v. 26). God was to receive glory through Shem. This was eventually fulfilled in the perfection of the Messiah, Jesus Christ the Lord. The Lord Jesus speaks of this, "I have glorified thee on the earth" (John 17:4). Eventually the nation of Israel, descendants of Shem, will be to the glory of God with Christ their head in the coming millennium.

In passing, how delightful it is to see that the gospel levels all. In the three conversion stories in Acts 8-10 one springs from each of the three sons of Noah. The man from Ethiopia in Acts 8 was a descendant of Ham, Saul of Tarsus being a Jew sprang from Shem (Acts 9), and Cornelius whose conversion story, so enjoyable to read, is recorded in Acts 10, originated from Japheth.

So we end the search of these great four chapters of Genesis. We have sought to follow the steps of Peter who first drew attention to the way in which the flood, and its details, displayed the glory and nature of God. Likely, all that has been noticed was gleaned also by Peter, and perhaps much more which is not recorded.

28

A DISPENSATIONAL PICTURE

It is time to approach our final chapter, the substance of which is the dispensational picture seen in the history of Noah and the flood. It is evident that there is a dispensational setting in the record of the flood from the following:

The fact that Peter draws parallels between the judgment of the flood, and the final judgment of the last days (2 Pet 3).

The Lord likens the days of Noah to the days that precede the coming of the Son of man.

The nations and their future character are dealt with at the close of the history of Noah (Gen 9-10).

The system of days that is noted in the whole story of the ark and the flood.

The fact that all is brought to a climax in the last book of the Bible, the Revelation.

This final book mentions many things that are first noted in the flood history, teaching us that the programme of the purposes of God in the last days is unfolded in Genesis 6-9 as well as in the Revelation. The Bible ends as it begins, and many comparisons between Genesis and Revelation have often been made. To complete our subject it will be necessary to list the links between the flood record and the Revelation.

NOAH

(1) The ark and its measurements are the first such details recorded in the Bible. The last measurements on record are found in Revelation 21, and are those of the New Jerusalem.

(2) The violence and corruption of Noah's day are seen headed up in the beast of violence (Rev 13) and the corruption of the scarlet woman (Rev 17).

(3) The sons of God of Genesis 6, if we take them to be angels, and their mingling with women have their counterpart in Revelation 8-9. Millions of demons will be at large upon the earth, fallen angels. Among other things, they will have hair like a woman's. Also there are the 144000 who have not defiled themselves with women, virgins unto the Lord, although the emphasis no doubt is upon spiritual faithfulness (Rev 14).

(4) The door of the ark and the voice "Come thou... into the ark" correspond with Revelation 4. A door is opened in heaven and the voice calls John to come up hither.

(5) The flood from God that succeeded in wiping out the ungodly can be contrasted with the flood from the mouth of the dragon that failed to wipe out the godly (Rev 12).

(6) The invitation to come into the ark can be linked with the last invitation in the Bible, "and the Spirit and the bride say, Come" (Rev 22:17). Both invitations are from divine persons, and they are the first and last invitations in the Bible.

(7) Similarly, the first altar in the Bible is in Genesis 8 and the last is in Revelation 8. In both the offerings are sweet savour offerings.

(8) The raven sent forth and content to feed on the carcasses of people drowned in the flood is parallel with the call to the fowls of the air to feed upon the flesh of kings and captains (Rev 19). Both episodes occur after a judgment by God.

A DISPENSATIONAL PICTURE

(9) The rain from heaven that lead to the terrible flood is akin to the great hail each stone of which weighed a talent (Rev 16). Both are the judgment of God, but rain in Scripture is more usually linked with blessing.

(10) The first and last vineyards are found in the two records, that planted by Noah (Gen 9) and the vine of the earth. The blood of the grape has its parallel in the blood that came out of the winepress even unto the horses bridles (Rev 14:19-20).

(11) Noah, the first man in the Bible to be drunken, is alongside the scarlet woman drunken with the blood of saints and martyrs of Jesus (Rev 17:6).

(12) Noah's literal nakedness is parallel with the moral nakedness referred to in Revelation 3:18. The Lord was able to provide white raiment that they of Laodicea might be clothed, then the shame of their nakedness would not appear. In Genesis 9 the covering came from the sons, in Revelation 3 it comes from the Lord. In both cases it covered nakedness. The reference in Revelation 16:15 is also important, "Blessed is he that... keepeth his garments, lest he walk naked, and they see his shame". This is the very thing in which Noah failed.

(13) The bow in the cloud (Gen 8) and the beautiful emerald bow encircling the throne of God (Rev 4) both speak of the faithfulness of God to His promises.

(14) The development of Babylon commences in Genesis 10-11 and finds its culmination in Revelation 17-18. Here we have the beginning and the end of Satan's religious kingdom.

(15) The curse, mentioned three times in the history of Noah is finally removed (Rev 22:3): "the ground which the Lord has cursed" (Gen 5:29); "I will not again curse the ground any more for man's sake" (Gen 8:21); "Cursed be Canaan" (Gen 9:25); "there shall be no more curse" (Rev 22:3).

Most agree that Revelation is a dispensational book, having to do with future times and seasons, the consummation of the purpose of God in relation to the Jew, the Gentiles and the church of God. From the many connections between the narrative of the flood and this prophetic book, one can rightly conclude that the flood is dispensational in character. The task now is to summarise these features in the flood history.

1. The condition of the then world, full of violence and corruption on an unprecedented scale, demanded the judgment of God. The rising of a man, Lamech, who is violent and defiant of the laws of God, is a foreshadowing of the coming of the beastly king of the last days.

2. Prior to the full manifestation of evil, Enoch the man who walked with God was raptured. It will be so with the true church. Perhaps Paul had Enoch in mind in 1 Thessalonians 4. He began that chapter with the exhortation that we ought "to walk and to please God", the very words used of Enoch. At the end of the chapter he revealed the rapture of the church to meet the Lord in the air, of which Enoch's was a foregleam. The middle of the chapter describes the ungodly among whom they were to walk, so like the days of Enoch and Noah.

3. Noah is a picture of the remnant of Israel, called of God. He was a preacher of righteousness. The task of the remnant in the last days will be to proclaim the gospel of the kingdom. He was preserved through the judgment flood, just as Israel will be preserved through the great tribulation. The little remnant standing on the top of Ararat, prefigures the 144000 who are to stand with the Lord on Mount Sion.

4. Through Noah others were saved and blessed, notably his three sons and their wives who became the progenitors of the Gentile nations (Gen 10-11). Even so

A DISPENSATIONAL PICTURE

through Israel a great number of Gentiles shall be saved, and all peoples of the earth blessed in the coming kingdom.

5. The predetermined period of judgement is measured in days (Gen 7:4,10-12). Even so, the tribulation is determined by God to last exactly 1260 days; the duration of both the flood and the tribulation is in His hands.

6. The flood was the hand of God in retribution for the sins of the people. Peter uses this as an assurance of the future judgment by means of fire in the day of the Lord.

7. There was no escape other than in the ark. Agreeing with this Paul says of sinners in the last days, "they shall not escape" (1 Thess 5:3). Again, "Thinkest thou...that thou shalt escape the judgment of God?" (Rom 2:3).

8. Noah coming out of the ark into a new world and erecting his altar, is, in type, Israel coming out of the tribulation into the blessing and prosperity of the millennium. The vineyard of Noah's planting also speaks of blessing in the coming age.

9. Noah prefigures Israel in her rightful place as head of the nations. Seedtime and harvest foreshadow the prosperity of the kingdom. The establishment of government points forward to that of the Lord Jesus when rightousness shall reign. The everlasting covenant shall be made good to Israel. However, sin shall still be present, as in Noah and Ham, but judgment will be immediately executed. All is based upon sacrifice, both in the types and in the reality. The Lord tasted death for everything. Presently, the whole creation groans waiting for the liberty of the sons of God. All awaits this consummation (Rom 8).

10. The doom of Canaan, the demise of the posterity of Japheth and the supremacy of the sons of Shem at the end of Genesis 9, prefigure the end of the millennial age. The enemies shall go into eternal perdition, the blessed into the eternal day of God.

NOAH

One final word. At the close of the Genesis 9 we read, "All the days of Noah were nine hundred and fifty years and he died". What a life to leave on record! what a man! well could he die and leave such giant footsteps behind. He died to enter triumphantly into the presence of the God whom he served so energetically, faithfully and fully. May there be many this day who will emulate him. The world, soon to enter into judgment, stands in need of many with the earnestness of Noah.

THE END